PLANT-BASED
HIGH-PROTEIN COOKBOOK

122 Ready-to-go, Delicious & Easy High-Protein Vegan Recipes for Athletic Performance & Muscle Growth. Burn Fat and Boost Your Energy & Vitality for a Healthy Lifestyle

MELANY CARTER

Copyright 2019 by **MELANY CARTER** - All rights reserved.

This document is geared towards providing exact and reliable information with regard to the topic and issue covered. The publication is sold with the idea that the publisher is not required to render accounting, officially permitted, or otherwise, qualified services. If advice is necessary, legal or professional, a practiced individual in the profession should be ordered.

From a Declaration of Principles which was accepted and approved equally by a Committee of the American Bar Association and a Committee of Publishers and Associations.

In no way is it legal to reproduce, duplicate, or transmit any part of this document in either electronic means or in printed format. Recording of this publication is strictly prohibited and any storage of this document is not allowed unless with written permission from the publisher.

Table Of Contents

Introduction 1
Chapter 1 2
The Protein Requirements 2
    Vegetable Protein Diet: Do Vegetable Proteins Contain All The Essential Amino Acids? 3
    How Many Proteins Do You Really Need? 5
    How To Calculate Your Protein Requirements? 5
    Let's Take A Few Practical Examples 6
Chapter 2 7
Why Choose A Vegan Diet? 7
    14 Benefits Of A Vegan Diet 8
Chapter 3 11
Breakfast Recipe 11
    1. Porridge 11
    2. Plumcake Choco And Orange 12
    3. Larr Cake 12
    4. Morning Brioches 13
    5. Pancake Almond And Quinoa 13
    6. Overnight 14
    7. Brioches Of The Sun 14
    8. Delicious Cake 15
    9. Pancake 15
    10. Pancake Recipe 2 16
    11. Porridge Of The Heart 16
    12. Water-Based Plumcake 17
    13. Pancake Recipe 4 17
    14. Pumpkin Spice 17
    15. Banana Milk Pan Pannier Case 18
    16. French Toast 19
    17. Raisin Swivels 19
    18. Raspberry Scented Brioches 20
    19. Nuvelle 20
    20. Dark Biscuit 21
Chapter 4 22
Lunch Recipe 22
    1. Ragu Of Lentils 22
    2. Pasta With Purple Cabbage Pesto 23

3. Pasta With Flowers And Herbs 23
   4. Apple Dumplings 24

Chapter 5 26
Recipes For Main Courses And Single Dishes 26
   1. Aubergines Meatballs 26
   2. Tofu With Pizzaiola Sauce 27
   3. Vegatorella 27
   4. Seitan Greenery 29
   5. Tempeh Leek And Pepper 30
   6. Tofu With Shoots 30
   7. Seitan In Spicy Sauce 31
   8. Farifrittata 31
   9. Almonds And Carrots Patties 31
   10. Curry Soya Stew 32
   11. Seitan Medallions 32
   12. Soya Escalope 33
   13. Zucchini And Tofu Skewers 33
   14. Breaded Slices Of Seitan 34
   15. Happy Chicken Tempeh 34
   16. Spicy Tofu With Cauliflower 35
   17. Seitan Tonnato 35
   18. Mopur 36
   19. Pumpkin Soya Stew 36
   20. Polpettone 37
   21. Soia 37
   22. Wheat Muscle In Stew 38
   23. Soya And Eggplant Morsels 38
   24. Slap In The Face 39
   25. Chickpeas And Spinach With Andalusian Sauce 39
   26. Chickpea Meatballs And Yoghurt Sauce 40
   27. Burger Pumpinks 41
   28. Rye And Wholemeal Oats With Garden Flowers 41
   29. Chickpeas, Cauliflowers, Tamari And Yoghurt Sauce 42
   30. Millet And Red Turnips 43
   31. Triangles Delight 43
   32. Sorghum And Lentils 44
   33. Bean Meatballs 45
   34. Legume Olives 45
   35. Spelt And Coconut Salad 46
   36. Bean And Rosemary Chips 47
   37. Meatloaf Of Legumes 47
   38. Zuppa Has Profumi Of Orientation 48
   39. Fonio Meatballs And Vegetables 48
   40. Hummus Black 49
   41. Pumpkin And Black Cabbage Rice 50

Chapter 6 51
Self-Produced Veg Sliced Meats 51

1. Veg Salsiccia 51
2. Sliced Soya Beans 51
3. Salamini Veg 52
4. Yubacetta 53
5. Sliced With Seitan And Lentils 53
6. Salamel 54
7. Mopur 55
8. Soyacetta 55
9. Tofucetta 56
10. Yoba Salami 57
11. Yellow Salami 57
12. Barbos 58
13. Wurstel 60
14. White Dinner 60
15. Sliced With Lentils 61
16. Salami Wonder 62
17. Wurstel Type 2 63
18. Trasure Dinner 64
19. Salami Red 65
20. Smoked Salami 66
21. Homemade Salami 67
22. Trust Dinner 67
23. Salami With Puttanesca Cheese 68
24. Fairy Salami 69
25. Sliced Happy 70

Chapter 7 72
Vegan Cheese 72

1. Stracchino Veg 72
2. Coccola 72
3. Tris 73
4. Raw Cheese 74
5. Tofu 74
6. Pumpkin Seed Cheese 75
7. Veg Recipe 75
8. Vegcheese 76
9. Almond Spreadable Cheese 76
10. Soya Ricotta 77
11. Moncaprice 77
12. Tofulino 78
13. Canestrato Veg 79
14. Veggrana 79
15. Mozzarella's Veg 80

16. Coccocaciotta 80
17. Mandorella 81
18. Pumpkin Tofuricotta 81
19. Vegalpino 82
20. Flower Malga 82
21. Cashew Mozzarella 83
22. Philadelpi Veg 84
23. Sottilfette 84
24. Veg Cheese Sage And Walnuts 85
25. Fiordoro 85
26. Tofulivella 86
27. Tarragon 86
28. Cacilette 87
29. Radicamaro 88
30. Condicacio 89
31. Lupis 89
32. Casu 90

Conclusions 91

INTRODUCTION

We grew up in steaks and glasses of milk, the emblem of a diet rich in protein and essential for growth, and after the Dukan diet, we greeted the carbohydrates, in the name of the line. But there are not only meat, fish, and dairy products, there are many other proteins in legumes, seeds, and cereals. All carbo-phobic: the protein diet (but vegetarian).

Proteinsare Not All The Same

To feel good it is necessary to consume the right amount of protein every day, without these being necessarily of animal origin - explains the Umberto Veronesi Foundation - proteins are not all the same. They are divided into animal proteins and vegetable proteins: the former are rich in essential amino acids but are generally found in foods that also contain saturated fats and cholesterol.

Lentils, chickpeas, beans, peas, lentils, broad beans and soya, cereals such as quinoa and spelt and many oilseeds are a mine of proteins, and if combined together in recipes such as pasta and beans and rice and peas, they complement each other, meeting the daily needs of an individual. 30g of lentils or peanuts, combined with bread or rice, for example, contain more protein than a hamburger or a pork steak and can replace the classic "slice" several times a week.

A Protein Diet

A healthy and balanced diet requires a protein requirement (indicated by FAO and WHO) of about 1g per kilo of body weight, then about 60g for an adult of 60k, i.e., proteins must occupy 10-15% of the diet. A diet rich in protein means having a wealth of energy for the body, but a hyper-protein diet can instead cause serious damage to the kidneys, which must dispose of the excess consumption.

This is all the more so when it comes to a slimming diet. Protein should be taken regularly throughout the day, alternating between carbohydrate and protein-rich meals and snacks. This is also the opinion of the New Food Pyramid developed by INRAN, which now recommends an equal consumption of animal and vegetable proteins in the diet.

High Company

Legumes with the same weight as meat are much more satiating and less caloric because their water content is high and this means a feeling of greater satisfaction during meals and in the medium term.

Protein Breakfast

Breakfast on certain days of the week can also be protein-rich, as can a mid-morning snack if you have already consumed a dose of carbohydrates. Legumes at this stage of the day are not welcome, but yogurt, dried fruit, and oilseeds such as sunflower, flax, sesame, and pumpkin) are an excellent sweet solution.

CHAPTER 1

THE PROTEIN REQUIREMENTS

Vegan protein diet: protein and vegan diet

Protein requirements, especially when it comes to the vegan diet, is a topic that ignites the most heated debates because there is still a lot of fear about consuming a few proteins.

If you, like us, want to see clearly once and for all how much protein you need in your vegan diet, then in this article you will find out how to ensure that you get all the proteins you need (and even more) with a vegan protein diet and how to calculate your protein requirement.

We want to talk to you about our experience free from iron ideologies, which clashes with both lines of thought, but that we are sure will finally help you get a clear idea on the issue of protein and vegan diet.

The protein requirement is the amount of protein that our body needs to meet its energy needs and maintain good health.

Let's say right away that these quantities vary depending on some factors such as:

- age;
- sex;
- work activity;
- sport activity.

Proteins help to ensure essential functions such as fluid balance, blood clotting, cell repair and construction, production of hormones and enzymes, and vision.

Proteins are similar to carbohydrates and lipids in that each molecule contains atoms of carbon, oxygen, and hydrogen.

The main difference is that proteins also contain nitrogen, which makes up about 16% of the molecule, and the official protein requirement is calculated by measuring the excretion of nitrogen.

From this, an average daily loss of 33 grams of protein has been calculated.

Taking into account other factors such as digestibility and absorption, it was officially estimated that there was 0.8 gram of protein per kg of body weight.

We can understand, however, that even official estimates are to be taken with the pliers because they are general and not reliable from a subjective point of view.

However, if we want to keep this result for the moment, how can vegans be sure to get all the proteins from the diet, or better yet, the right amount of essential amino acids?

Vegetable Protein Diet: Do Vegetable Proteins Contain All The Essential Amino Acids?

There are 20 food amino acids, of which 8 are known as essential amino acids (EAA).

These are essential because (in theory this is what official science tells us), they can only be obtained from the food taken, and the body cannot produce them from other amino acids and proteins.

If you do not get it from the diet, the body will try to synthesize it by degrading the skeletal muscle, another process called muscle protein catabolism (the opposite of catabolism is anabolism, hence the anabolic body building).

Here we insert the photograph extracted from a typical nutritional day according to the Health & Vegan program and which shows the percentages of the various amino acids in relation to the official recommendations:

Protein		
Protein	126.5 g	226%
Cystine	1.4 g	397%
Histidine	3.1 g	356%
Isoleucine	4.5 g	257%
Leucine	7.7 g	228%
Lysine	5.8 g	224%
Methionine	1.1 g	125%
Phenylalanine	4.8 g	439%
Threonine	4.0 g	306%
Tryptophan	1.0 g	282%
Tyrosine	3.5 g	319%
Valine	4.8 g	212%

Consider that this food day represents a period of muscular construction of a thirty-year-old man (therefore with consumption of many calories), but it is clear that all amino acids are clearly in surplus with respect to the official recommendations.

This means that vegans do not have to eat cereals (lacking in tryptophan and lysine) and legumes (lacking in methionine and cysteine) at the same time, but they can simply eat one at lunch and the other at dinner.

What we would like to share with you is the fact that the myth of essential amino acids has been strongly questioned for decades by Professor D'Elia "Myths and realities of human nutrition".

At the International Congress on Proteins held in Bern, Professor A. Abelin even denied that essential amino acids are indispensable in food intended for humans, stating that they can be synthesized by the human body, such as non-essential amino acids.

Through clinical investigations, these essential amino acids have been found in sufficient quantities even in individuals whose food was totally devoid of them.

The well-known Prof. E. Schneider comments on this sensational news:

"This discovery has demolished everything that until now was believed to know about protein metabolism because it has shown that it does not matter the type of protein absorbed since the living cell is able to use any food that contains protein, then building independently those compounds that the body needs specific.

This concept, according to which the body would be able to obtain substances considered essential through internal transformations and oxidation, is not new.

When we talk about protein and vegan protein diet we talk a lot about animal and vegetable proteins in comparison, but we should rather talk about the amino acids contained, which are the substances that are really absorbed.

Our body is not able to recognize where an amino acid comes from once it has been broken down, the real problem lies in the digestion of proteins.

Those animals require a lot more energy to be broken up and carry with them toxic acidifying and inflammatory waste that should not enter the human body:

- CADAVERIC ALCALOIDS (Cathol, Indole, Cadaverine, Putrescine);
- METABOLIC WASTE AND TOXIC AMINES;
- URICO AND AMONICA ACIDUM (Extremely Acidifying);
- ADRENALINE ACCUMULATED AT THE TIME OF DEATH;
- PESTICIDES AND DIOXINS...

Not to mention the saturated fats present at the same time in meat, cheese, milk, and eggs.

You can see that in vegetable foods saturated fats and cholesterol are non-existent or almost non-existent...

As far as red meat is concerned, on the other hand, it has an amino acid composition with a strong presence of branched amino acids and a ratio between methionine and cysteine that accelerate the oxidation of the mitochondria (by translating, they develop the muscles more quickly, but also cause the cell to age quickly).

How Many Proteins Do You Really Need?

Science has so far established protein requirements for health between 0.8 and 1.4 grams of protein per kg of body weight.

Here we want to talk about 2 different ways of seeing the protein issue, one official, the other concerning the hygienist science.

The current guidelines of the Institute of Medicine set the protein RDA at 0.8 g/kg and consider it valid for 97% of the population; The American school of hygiene or Dr. Adolfo Panfili speaks instead of the risks of acidification arising from a protein quota that exceeds even 30 / 40 grams of protein per day.

Campbell himself warns against exceeding the protein quota and adheres with his studies to a 10% of protein calculated on the daily caloric requirement.

It is interesting to note the escalation of the Food and Drug Administration, which in recent decades has significantly reduced the amount of protein recommended: In the 70's the FDA pushed on 300 grams of noble proteins per day (steaks for breakfast, lunch, snack, and dinner).

In the 1980s, the FDA was pushed to take more gentle advice and preached 250 grams a day.

In the 1990s, it fell to 200 under pressure.

In 2000, frightened by the Cambridge experiment, she retouched to 150.

In 2005, she was asked to level 100.

Today, almost squeezed by thousands of studies and demonstrations of the danger of hyperprotective diets, it remains at level 75!

How To Calculate Your Protein Requirements?

Here, we want to share with you not only data but also our direct personal experience of over 6 years as semi-crudist vegans and members of our Health & Vegan program.

We have adhered for a long time to hygienist theories and have never noticed any kind of deficiency or difficulty of any kind or energy deficiency, quite the contrary!

What we have noticed, however, is that a protein quota of 10% is optimal for sedentary adults or for those who have a pathology in progress and want to restore a basic acid balance in their bodies (so avoid at most exceeding with proteins).

We have noticed, instead, that for sportsmen and growing children the daily protein quota can easily be around 20%, without any problem, but that, on the contrary, a greater supply of vegetable and raw proteins helps the development of muscle mass.

Let's Take A Few Practical Examples

For a 40-year-old woman, who is healthy with the aim of maintaining her youth for as long as possible and is sedentary, weighing 55 kg and 168 cm tall, her protein requirement can be as high as 10% to 15%.

1800 calories ==> 15% = approximately 50 - 60 grams of protein

For a healthy 40-year-old man, with the aim of maintaining lean mass and youth and sedentary, with a weight of 80 kg and a height of 180 cm, his protein requirement (between 10% and 15%) could be:

2500 calories ==>15% = approximately 80 - 90 grams of protein

We would like to point out that in practice when you go on a semi-crudist vegan diet that provides all the energy you need, you will also take the proteins necessary for your daily protein turnover. That's why the vegan protein diet is nothing more than a healthy, nutritious, and healthy vegan diet.

Here we've talked about the protein needs of "normal" people who don't practice regular and intensive sports; next week we'll be publishing a detailed article for vegan and protein sportsmen.

In the next article, we will explain how to organize your sports nutrition and get the most out of your strength, performance, and muscle mass (including protein).

If you still don't think it's possible to build lean vegan mass, then don't miss the next newsletter.

Basically, if you follow our practical Alkaline Plant Nutrition program, the only things you'll have to be careful of are:

Choose the right plant foods (fruits, vegetables, seeds, nuts, cereals, and legumes); combine them well; eat enough to support your energy needs,

and the protein issue will be automatically resolved; no deficiency, no excess, acid-base balance under control, and prevention of future diseases ensured!

CHAPTER 2

WHY CHOOSE A VEGAN DIET?

Why become a vegan? More and more people are choosing to change their diet and opt for a cruelty-free lifestyle, i.e. free from any kind of cruelty to other living beings. This growing awareness has prompted, according to the latest Eurispes statistics, 8% of Italians to choose to become vegetarian or vegan (7.1% and 1% respectively). But what does it mean to be vegan? And what are the pros and cons of becoming a vegan?

In this article we will try to explain why becoming a vegan is now a choice not only possible but also preferable and advisable, for ourselves, for animals, and for the entire planet, because eating vegan is good for everyone: here are therefore 14 good reasons to become a vegan.

What does a vegan eat? Easy!

The first question we ask when we talk about "vegans" is: but what do they eat?

In many cases, the Western lifestyle and diet have led, in recent decades, to excessive daily consumption of foods of animal origin, meat, cheese, and eggs in the first place, and thinking of eliminating these "cornerstones" of the daily diet seems to most a crazy decision, to say the least. This is in fact one of the first obstacles to be overcome when one wonders how to become a vegan.

Nothing could be more wrong. A vegan diet, even if devoid of any food of animal origin, is very rich in various healthy foods. Cereals, legumes, fruits, and vegetables, especially if eaten according to their seasonality, make it possible to cover the recommended need of all nutrients.

Because becoming vegan also means learning to combine foods and spices belonging to culinary traditions of other continents, aromas and flavors that are increasingly widespread here too and that allow us to follow an increasingly rich diet, just as it will be possible to replace foods such as milk and cheese with others that are similar but derived from vegetable products and by far poorer in saturated fats.

In the near future we will talk in more detail about the many foods that make up a vegan diet, in the meantime let's see why we become vegans.

14 Benefits Of A Vegan Diet

1. Reduced intake of saturated fats: Saturated and transidrogenated fats are those most often responsible for heart disease. A vegan diet is far lower in saturated fat than an omnivorous diet, as most saturated fat is contained in meat and dairy products.

   Becoming vegan involves the elimination of these foods and the replacement of saturated fats with unsaturated fats (olive oil, linseed oil, walnuts, avocado), and it is a fundamental step to reducing the risk of heart disease. Needless to say, moreover, thanks to the reduced intake of saturated fats associated with a healthy lifestyle and not being sedentary, becoming vegan makes you lose weight, or can still help you lose weight;

2. High levels of fiber: Fruits and vegetables are naturally rich in fiber, invaluable to our intestines, and able to reduce the risk of colon cancer. Any vegan recipe has a much higher fiber content than a dish made from products of animal origin and their intake in the right doses can only bring benefits to the entire gastrointestinal tract;

3. High presence of antioxidants: Many plant foods are rich in antioxidants, substances that can slow down cellular aging by preventing the phenomena of oxidation and the formation of free radicals. Berries, spices, and dried fruit, are just some of the types of foods richer in antioxidants, as we explained in our previous article: the best antioxidant foods;

4. Reduced risk of cardiovascular disease and hypertension: The consumption of whole foods and dried fruit, the latter rich in omega-3 fats, normalizes blood pressure and reduces the risk of heart attack and stroke. Numerous studies have now demonstrated the relationship between the intake of omega-3 fats and benefits for the heart and arteries: these substances are, in fact, able to prevent cardiovascular disease, hindering the formation of atherosclerotic plaque and blood clots, lowering the level of triglycerides and blood pressure;

5. Reduction of the risk of cancer: Also in this case, since meat and dairy products are responsible for different types of cancer, the elimination of these products from the diet reduces the risks for these diseases;

6. Reduction of the risk of type 2 diabetes: A study published in recent months in Plos Medicine, a journal of the Harvard School of Public Health in Boston, has confirmed that a diet based on vegetables, provided it is free of drinks and sugary foods, is able to reduce the risk of type 2 diabetes. The research, which lasted 20 years, has in practice shown that fibers, antioxidants, unsaturated fatty acids, and micronutrients contained in plant foods, play a key role in the prevention of this disease;

7. Reduced impact of allergies: The most common allergies occur due to the intake of products of animal origin and their elimination allows for clear improvements in the respiratory system.

8. Less waste of resources: Among the consequences of the vegan choice, there is certainly less consumption of water, energy, pesticides, and drugs, as well as land and, consequently, less deforestation. Just think that the

meat sector is now one of the most polluting and that 20% of the CO2 emitted into the atmosphere comes from farms. What about the consumption of water, an increasingly precious and endangered commodity? To produce 1 kg of meat, you need 3900 liters if it is chicken, about 6000 liters for pork, and even 15000 liters per 1 kg of beef, well beyond the average consumption expected for the same amount of a plant product. We also eat vegan to protect the environment!

9. Defending the marine ecosystem: The Sea Shepherd Conservation Society is a non-profit association that deals with the protection of marine life and environments. It is these good "pirates" who give us the scale of the drama that is being consumed in the seas and oceans around the globe.

    Indiscriminate fishing is in fact destroying the marine ecosystem, leading to the disappearance of many fish species, and, if there is no reversal in the current framework, it is plausible that by 2048 fishing activities will collapse due to the loss of biodiversity in the marine ecosystem.

    In addition, man-made pollution and marine litter (including from intensive farming) are likely to cause climate change and acidification of the oceans. About 80% of the oxygen we breathe comes from the oceans and, as Paul Watson, Captain of Sea Shepherd, says, "if the oceans die, we will die too".

10. More equitable redistribution of resources: "If everyone became a vegan, there would be no hunger in the world": it seems an exaggeration, yet such a strong statement is based on real data. To give a more concrete image, think that today the portion of land used to feed a person who consumes meat could produce food for about 20 vegan people. One hectare of land for cattle breeding will produce about 66 kg of protein in one year, compared to the 1868 kg that would be obtained by allocating the same space to a crop such as soya.

    Moreover, about one-third of the cereals produced all over the world are used for farm animals. It is clear that if the same quantity were destined for human consumption, that quantity would feed a much higher number of people than those for whom the meat produced instead is destined.

    For most vegans, the animalist question is perhaps the first spring that pushes towards this choice. A motivation that, perhaps, compared to the previous ones, is more evident even to non-vegans, even if we do not always have the real dimensions of the brutality hidden behind the breeding of animals. However, we would also like to briefly observe this last aspect and understand why becoming a vegan is also important for the protection of our animal friends.

11. Cruelty to animals: Today it is very easy to find on the internet videos that document more than any word what happens in intensive farming. Even before the killing of the animals themselves, which would already be enough to open a debate on the need to deprive a sentient being of life, the daily cruelty perpetrated on innocent souls has become something intolerable for anyone with a minimum of humanity.

In pig farms, for example, pregnant sows are placed in gestation cages that prevent any kind of movement, except to get up and down, on a concrete or wooden floor free of straw and litter, materials that the mother would instinctively use to build a shelter for her puppies.

The puppies, on the contrary, after a few days of life, are castrated without anesthesia in order not to prejudice the taste of the flesh; the tail is then amputated to them, in order to avoid that, in prey to the stress, the pigs bite each other, and the teeth are eradicated, in order to avoid damages to the nipples of the sow.

In the poultry industry, on the other hand, male chicks, which are considered unproductive, are eliminated without half measures and die by asphyxiation, beheading, grinding, or crushing. Not to mention the inhumane conditions in which chickens are forced to be reared for subsequent slaughter.

The condition of cattle is no better. Both beef and veal production and the production of milk and cheese involve violence against these peaceful animals. Just think of forced pregnancies, the removal of puppies from mothers a few days after birth, to be able to use the milk, until the killing at an early age of the same puppies destined to become meat for human consumption.

These are just a few examples, but many animal welfare organizations have now documented cruel and inhuman behavior in all types of farming, just look in the network to achieve the size of such a massacre. Can a dish justify so much violence?

12. Enabling animals to live according to their natural expectations: Meat production (but also dairy products and eggs) requires animals to be slaughtered much earlier than their natural life expectancy should be: a pig should live 20 years but is killed at 5 months of age; chickens, which would live 20 years, are slaughtered at 5-6 weeks; male chicks are eliminated within an hour of birth; the dairy cow could live 30 years but is sent to the slaughterhouse at around 5-7 years; and so on. Each of these animals would probably like its existence to follow the laws of nature.

13. To be more empathetic: Becoming a vegan can be a time to open up to greater empathy towards all other living beings. A 2010 study found that at the brain level "vegetarians and vegans have a higher activation of areas of the frontal lobe of the brain associated with the development and perception of empathic feelings". Beyond this, however, it is clear that those who choose not to feed themselves with violence develop a greater sensitivity to certain issues.

14. To open up to new aspects and new cultures: The vegan choice can also help to open one's mind to new topics, new situations, and new cultures, to get involved and get out of the schemes and habits with which one grew up. This is evident when we talk about food since we often find ourselves experimenting with new foods that were previously ignored and recipes from other areas of the world, but gradually this opening will also involve many other aspects of our lives, with all the benefits that follow. Try it to believe!

CHAPTER 3

BREAKFAST RECIPE

1. Porridge

The porridge has an ancient history and anyone who experiences the benefits of a breakfast with "oatmeal" no longer comes back. It is ideal, especially for those who find it hard not to get hungry at lunchtime or suffer from sugar drops: oats give us the great gift of energy well distributed over time, without glycemic peaks! Vegetable milk and other ingredients such as seeds and cinnamon reinforce the effect. For me it is also the comfort food par excellence: a naturally sweet food (without the need to add other sugars than those naturally present in the fruit) and creamy, to be eaten by the spoon!

This light version (without vegetable milk) I reserve for the weekend or holidays, when I get up later than usual I want a hearty breakfast but not too much.

Ingredients:

- Fresh fruit of your choice cut into pieces
- A bowl of oatmeal
- Half a banana
- Infusion of your choice according to your taste (I find that the delicacy of porridge goes very well with sweet or spicy infusions: blends of chamomile, flowers, cinnamon, cocoa peel but also red fruits and raspberry)
- Oilseeds (in particular pumpkin and sunflower seeds), Chia seeds
- Dehydrated fruit of your choice
- Cinnamon powder

Procedure:

a. Cut the fruit into pieces and put them together in a bowl (for this morning's porridge I used two slices of winter melon and two handfuls of blueberries).

b. In the meantime, prepare the infusion. I infused a mixture of lavender, chamomile flowers, mint, fennel, and lemon balm. Then pour the infusion, still warm, on the oat flakes. Let it rest for a few minutes to a few hours, depending on how creamy you want the soup to be.

2. Plumcake Choco And Orange

Ingredients:

- 9 oz of type 2 flour
- 2 oz of spelt flour
- 5 oz of cane sugar
- 8 oz of water
- 1½ oz of seed oil
- ½ oz of vegan yeast
- 1 oz of dark chocolate drops
- juice and peel of an untreated orange

Procedure:

a. Sift the flour with the yeast in a bowl. Add the chocolate drops and sugar, and stir. Add the oil and water, mix with a whisk and add the juice and rind of an untreated orange, mixing everything together.

b. Oil or line a plumcake mold with baking paper (you can also make muffins!), pour in the mixture, and bake in the oven at 180° for 40 minutes, always keeping an eye on cooking! Try it with a toothpick to make sure that the plumcake is well cooked. If you try it, let me know how you got it and if you like it! I love this recipe and I hope you will love it too.

3. Larr Cake

Ingredients:

- 11 oz of wholemeal spelt flour
- 5½ oz of whole cane sugar
- 11 fluid oz of almond milk
- 3 tablespoons of chopped flaxseed
- 1¾ oz of chopped almonds
- 3 tablespoons and 1 teaspoon of sesame oil (or sunflower oil as an alternative)
- 1 sachet of cremor tartar
- 1 handful of whole almonds
- 1 level teaspoon of ginger powder
- 1/2 bar of dark chocolate
- 3 apples

Procedure:

a. In a large bowl, add the almond milk (at room temperature), the oil, and the sugar. Mix with an electric whisk until the sugar begins to melt. Gradually add the sifted flour and cremor tartar and continue to mix with the whisk at low speed, so that no lumps are formed and until the dough is soft. Then add the chopped almonds and flaxseed. Peel the apples and form cubes to be incorporated into the dough, taking care to save a few slices to decorate the surface of the cake. Chop the dark chocolate in a coarse way and add it to the dough together with the ginger.

b. Mix everything very well. Cover a round cake pan with greaseproof paper (28 cm in diameter). You can then pour the dough into the cake pan. Decorate the surface of the cake with slices of apple and almonds in flakes. You can complete the decoration by adding a little chocolate, a sprinkling of sugar, and a drizzle of oil. Bake the cake and cook it for about 1 hour at 180°C. Help yourself with the "toothpick test" to see if it is cooked.

4. Morning Brioches

Ingredients:

- 7 oz of flour 0
- 1½ oz of wholemeal soft wheat flour
- 1/2 sachet of dried wheat sourdough
- 3½ oz of rice malt
- 1 fluid oz of sesame oil
- 1 teaspoonful of vanilla powder
- 1 pinch of whole sea salt
- Ingredients for icing:
- 1 teaspoon hazelnut cream (100% hazelnuts)
- 1 teaspoon of rice malt
- 1 tablespoon and 1 teaspoon of oat drink

Procedure:

a. Combine all the dry ingredients in a large bowl, mix and form a hole in the center. Combine oil and malt in a tall container and mix, then incorporate into the flours and knead to form a nice compact ball. Knead for another 5 minutes then place in the bowl, covering with a damp cloth, and put in the oven to rise with the only light on (without setting the temperature). Leave to rise overnight. In the morning take the dough and with the rolling pin form a disc as thin as possible. Cut the disc into 8 triangles and start to roll from the base of the triangle. At this point, if you want, you can insert a filling (such as jam or other sweet spreadable cream), I have left them empty. Once formed the "croissants," put them on the baking sheet, covered with a damp cloth, and let them rise for another 4 hours. Prepare an emulsion with the hazelnut cream, malt, and oat drink and brush the brioches. Then cook in the oven at 180° for about 20 minutes.

5. Pancake Almond And Quinoa

Ingredients:

- 3 tablespoons quinoa flour
- 3 tablespoons almond flour
- One tip of the handle of a tablespoon of cremor tartar
- A tip of the handle of a spoonful of baking soda

- 2 tablespoons homemade vegetable cream
- 1 tablespoon of apple butter
- Vegetable milk to taste

Procedure:

a. Add the dry ingredients and mix, then add the vegetal cream, mix, then add the milk until you get a dense and creamy mixture. I divided it into 4 segments because I wanted to try it with my homemade sauces: apple butter, hazelnut, and almond and I left a segment as it is.

6. Overnight

Ingredients:

- 1 jar of strawberry soya yogurt
- 1 oz of oat flakes
- 1 banana
- 1 tablespoon peanut butter
- cinnamon qb

Procedure:

a. The night before, in a cup, mix well the soya yogurt with the oatmeal and leave them to ferment in the fridge all night (I cover the mixture with a little film). In the morning, take out of the fridge your overnight (that's where the name comes from), cut a banana into slices and mix it, garnish with cinnamon at will and a giant spoonful of peanut butter. A faster, easier, and more complete breakfast is not possible... and I assure you that even the palate will be more than satisfied.

7. Brioches Of The Sun

Ingredients (for 4 medium-sized croissants or 8 mini croissants):

- 3 oz of wholemeal flour
- 4 oz of wholemeal spelt flour
- ¾ oz of cornstarch
- 3 oz of water
- 1¾ oz of vegetable oil
- 1½ oz of cane sugar
- 1 teaspoon cinnamon powder
- Vegetable chocolate spreadable cream

Procedure:

a. First, dissolve the sugar in the water and add it to the oil and cinnamon. Now pour the flours into a planetary mixer and start kneading, adding the liquids into the mixture little by little. Knead the mixture for at least 10 minutes until you get a ball well homogeneous and smooth that you have to let rest for at least 1/4 of an hour in the refrigerator. Once the dough has rested for the necessary time, place it on a pastry board and with the help of a rolling pin roll out the dough trying to give it a round shape and a thickness of 3-4 mm.

Using a knife, divide the disc obtained into 8 equal parts, thus obtaining 8 triangles that will be the base of your vegan croissants ready to be filled. For the filling, I have chosen a spreadable cream with vegetable chocolate, but you can also use jam. Start now to arrange with a teaspoon the filling at the base of the triangle and start to wrap the croissants on themselves proceeding towards the tip of the triangle thus obtaining the classic shape of the industrial croissants. To seal the croissants well before wrapping them around themselves, I suggest you brush the edges with a mixture of water and sugar. Repeat the process for all the croissants and do not exaggerate with the filling, otherwise it will drip away during cooking. Prepare all the vegan croissants, brush them with a little water and sprinkle with sugar, to obtain when cooking is completed a golden and tasty surface. Bake them in the oven for about 10 minutes at 180°, activating the grill function during the last minute of cooking to obtain a sweet and golden surface. Let me know what you think

8. Delicious Cake

Ingredients:

- 13 plums in syrup
- 11 tablespoons of their syrup
- 8 tablespoons rye flour
- 4 tablespoons of flour 00
- 1 teaspoon of baking soda
- 1 drop of plum liqueur (optional)
- 1 pinch of salt
- Juice of 1 squeezed orange
- 1 cup of coffee with little rice oil (or seed)

Procedure:

a. Let's remove the prunes in syrup and put them in the blender. Let's also add the orange juice and 11 tablespoons of their syrup, and mix everything until you get a puree, to which we will also add the oil.

b. Pour the mixture into a bowl containing the flour, salt, and baking soda and mix well to dissolve any lumps. We also incorporate the liqueur and mix again until it is absorbed, then pour the cream obtained in an oiled mold and lined with breadcrumbs and bake at 180° for 50 minutes. After the first 20 minutes of cooking, it is advisable to cover the mold with a steel lid or aluminium foil, to prevent the cake from darkening too much on the surface.

9. Pancake

Ingredients:

- 1 banana
- 3½ oz of wholemeal flour
- 2 handfuls of raisins
- 1 pinch of cinnamon

- 1 pinch of yeast
- Water qb
- 1 tablespoon of oil
- Sugar-free berry jam (or any other taste you prefer)

Procedure:

a. Crush the ripe banana and add the flour stirring, adding water to taste, until the dough has the right consistency. Add the oil and, finally, raisins, cinnamon, and yeast and continue to mix well the ingredients together. Proceed to the preparation of pancakes as always. Serve alternating layers of pancakes and layers of jam

10. Pancake Recipe 2

Ingredients:

- 3½ oz wholemeal flour
- 1/5 oz bitter cocoa
- Water qb
- 1 pinch of yeast
- Apricot jam (for me) qb

Procedure:

a. Prepare the batter of pancakes by mixing, and mixing well, the wholemeal flour, cocoa, yeast, and water, enough to obtain a dense dough, but not too much (go to the eye). On a hot non-stick frying pan, pour a generous spoonful of dough and when you see that it has thickened (because bubbles have formed on the edges), spread about 1/2 teaspoon of jam over the entire surface and cover with other dough. Turn and let cook also on the other side.

11. Porridge Of The Heart

Ingredients:

- 1¾ oz of boiled barley (kcal 46, kcal 92/100 g)
- 5 1/3 oz apple (kcal 78, kcal 52/100 g)
- 1/3 oz psyllium skin bran (kcal 20, kcal 200/100 g)
- 1/5 oz of chia seeds (kcal 24.3, kcal 486/100 g)
- 1/6 oz of bitter cocoa powder (kcal 11.88, kcal 396/100 g)
- 1/6 oz of cinnamon (kcal 7.41, kcal 247/100 g)
- ½ oz dried figs (kcal 40.16 , kcal 251/100 g)
- 1/3 oz of prunes (kcal 26.4, kcal 220/100 g)
- 1/3 oz Foś inulin (kcal 24.96, kcal 208/100 g)
- 1/5 oz of spirulina powder (kcal 14.5, kcal 290/100 g)
- 14 oz of water (I boil water from red beets)

Procedure:

a. Mix all the ingredients well, until the psyllium peels begin their thickening and "pudding" action. Then refrigerate for at least 1 hour, better 1 and 1/2 or 2, perfect time for a session of mindfulness yoga. In this time, the porridge will begin to firm up and take on consistency.

If you want, you can eat it as it is, cold. In my opinion, however, to be truly greedy, the apple must cook and the porridge takes on even more consistency and homogeneity by warming up. So off to the microwave, 950 W for 4 minutes, or until you bring it to first boiling, without exaggerating.

12. Water-Based Plumcake

Ingredients:

- 12½ oz of wholemeal flour
- 3 oz of cane sugar Mascobado
- 1 cup of water
- 1/3 cup of seed oil
- 1 sachet of cremor tartar (or yeast)
- 3 tablespoons of black sesame
- 3 tablespoons of white poppy seeds

Procedure:

a. Simply mix everything in a bowl and put in a plumcake mold. This time I also added 1 tablespoon of Mascobado sugar even over to make the crust, but it is not necessary. I bake at 180 degrees for about 30 minutes, but it depends on your oven, however, I always do the "toothpick test". Once cold it will be more compact, but it will remain a very soft plumcake that will last for several days.

13. Pancake Recipe 4

Ingredients:

- 3 cups of wholemeal flour
- 2 cups of coconut flour
- 1 pear
- 1 glass of soy milk
- 1 cup of seed oil

Procedure:

a. Cut the pear into small pieces and put it in the glass of the minipimer with the other ingredients and mix everything. The consistency will be perfect! And the beautiful thing is that there will be no need for sugar! Once the dough is ready, put a quantity on the hot pan and cook over medium-high heat for 2 minutes on the side. I stuffed them with strawberry jam and veg nutella! My mom asked me for them last night! Too happy for me!

14. Pumpkin Spice

Ingredients:

- 2/3 cup of vegetable milk (I used the one from rice)
- 1 cup of coffee
- 1 tablespoon pumpkin pulp already cooked

- 1 tablespoon maple syrup
- cinnamon qb
- nutmeg qb

Procedure:

a. Heat the milk in the microwave or in a saucepan. Pour it into the mixer, add the other ingredients, and blend. Transfer the drink to a cup. At this point, if you have a microwave, I suggest you heat everything up again for about 1/2 minute until it will form a kind of foam/rind on the surface. Serve with a sprinkling of cocoa or whipped cream with a pinch of cinnamon.

15. Banana Milk Pan Pannier Case

Ingredients:

- 9 oz of manitoba flour
- 7 oz of wholemeal flour
- 1 cup of banana soy milk
- 1 sachet of dry brewer's yeast
- Barley powder qb
- 2 oz of sultanas
- 1 teaspoon stevia

Procedure:

a. First let's dissolve the sachet of dry yeast in the milk at room temperature (better if warm, the yeast melts better and earlier). Weigh all the ingredients carefully, then in a large bowl mix the flours with the soy milk and the yeast now dissolved: I had to decant the mixture in a pastry board to be able to better knead it. After all the ingredients are mixed, add the teaspoon of stevia (the first time I use it, but I was curious to see the result ... especially in desserts!). We continue to knead until we get a soft and smooth dough (having added during the preparation 1 tablespoon of barley powder, I had to add a drop of water, to make the dough softer). Let's put the mixture in the bowl used at the beginning (still floured, at least it doesn't stick), covering it with a cloth: let it rise for at least 3 hours, 3 hours, and 1/2. The dough must have reached at least twice its initial volume! Once this rising time has elapsed, we reshuffle the mixture together with the raisins. Place the final mixture in the plumcake mold (possibly made of silicone, like the one I used), leaving it to rest for another 2 hours. Before informing I wet the surface with soy milk, dusting then more barley powder. Unfortunately, I don't have an oven in my university house: if you are luckier, bake the bread for about 30 minutes at 180*, if you only have a microwave oven, let it cook for 8-10 minutes at the third power (250w). Wait a few minutes before removing it from the oven (or microwave). Once out of the oven, let it cool down and only then remove it from its shape! And here's to you a sweet, soft pan pannier, perfect for breakfast

16. French Toast

Ingredients:

- 1/2 glass of pumpkin puree
- 1/2 glass of vegetable milk
- 1 teaspoon of cornstarch
- 1 teaspoon cinnamon
- 1 pinch of turmeric
- Grated peel of 1/1 orange
- Oil qb (for frying)
- 3 small stale sandwiches

Procedure:

a. Add and mix all the ingredients together until you get a smooth batter. Cut each sandwich into 5 slices. Heat the oil in a non-stick pan (remember that it must be very, very hot before you start to fry your toast). Soak each side of the slice in pumpkin batter, then fry for 1/2 minute on one side and 1/2 minute on the other (or until they become golden). Serve on a serving plate accompanied by a little maple syrup, fresh fruit, icing sugar, or fruit jam - I usually choose the first option.

17. Raisin Swivels

Ingredients:

- 5 1/3 oz of freshened sourdough
- 5 1/3 oz of lukewarm water
- 7 oz of flour 0
- 7 oz of wholemeal flour
- 3 oz of cane sugar
- 1 tablespoon barley malt
- 2½ oz of corn oil
- 1 teaspoon bourbon vanilla
- Grated peel of 1 lemon
- 1 generous handful of raisins
- Apricot jam
- 1 pinch of salt

Procedure:

a. Mix all the ingredients in the planetary mixer except the raisins and jam, or by hand in a bowl, for at least 15 minutes, putting the oil last. Let the dough rise until it doubles, about 4 hours, in a glass bowl.

b. Then roll out the dough with a rolling pin in a rectangle 1/2 cm high. Brush the rectangle of dough with the jam and sprinkle with raisins. Then roll it up on itself from the shortest side and with a very sharp smooth blade knife cut off the swivels of a thickness of 3-4 cm. Turn the swivels and place them on a baking sheet with baking paper, let them rise all night and in the morning bake them in a preheated oven at 180° for 20 minutes. To me, with these doses have come out 20 swivels.

18. Raspberry Scented Brioches

Ingredients:

- 18 oz of mixed flour (I used 9 oz of wholemeal flour and 9 oz of flour 00)
- 9 oz of water (you can make 1/2 water and 1/2 veg milk, but I didn't have any)
- 1 sachet of dry brewer's yeast
- 1 cup of malt
- 5 1/3 oz of sugar
- 2 oz of oil
- Jam at will (my was raspberry, homemade)

Procedure:

a. In a bowl put the lukewarm liquids with the yeast and malt and dissolve. In a bowl mix the dry ingredients (flour and sugar). Slowly add the liquids and knead until you get a nice soft and smooth dough, but not sticky. Cover with blankets and let rise for 2 hours. After the necessary time, the dough will be doubled, roll it out with a rolling pin to form a sheet of dough of 1/2 cm, and cut into squares of about 3 cm per side. At this point take 1 square put 1 teaspoon of jam and close sealing with your fingers, forming balls. Cover the sandwiches with blankets and leave to rise for another 1 hour. After the resting time, bake for 15 minutes at 180° or until it is golden brown.

19. Nuvelle

Ingredients:

- 4 oz of wholemeal flour
- 3½ oz of wholemeal manitoba flour
- 1 oz of rice flour
- 2¾ oz of sourdough freshened the night before
- 1½ oz of corn oil
- 2 cup of barley malt
- 1/2 cup of turmeric
- 2½ oz lukewarm rice milk
- Lukewarm water qb
- Jam at will

Procedure:

a. First, dissolve the pm in a bowl with the milk and barley malt. Add the flours, turmeric, and oil and mix the ingredients well together. Add a pinch of salt and, if necessary, very little water. The dough should be soft and smooth. Work it a little, wrap it in a cloth and let it rise in a warm place. I always put the doughs that have to grow in the warm, off oven. After 3 hours. the dough will be well leavened, work it for a moment and peel off pieces of dough as large as a mandarin-shaped pallets, crush them slightly, and put in the center of each 1 teaspoon of jam. Close the lid by bending the edges of the dough toward the center so as to cover the filling. Let them rise like this, for another 2 hours. Then turn on the oven to 180° and cook for 8-10 minutes.

20. Dark Biscuit

Ingredients:

- 3½ oz of flour 00
- 3 oz of wholemeal flour
- 3½ oz of rice flour
- 1 oz of cornstarch
- 1½ oz carob flour
- 1½ oz of dehydrated coconut
- 3 oz of whole cane sugar Sweetened
- 1 cup satin bicarbonate
- 2 cups of chopped hazelnuts
- 2 tablespoons and 2 teaspoons of Evo oil
- Hot raw milk hazelnuts qb

Procedure:

In a large bowl, mix all the dry ingredients together. Add the chopped hazelnuts and stirring, add the oil and the raw Nocciolatte just enough until you get a soft and smooth dough. Wrap it in film and keep in the refrigerator for 40 minutes. Take the dough and roll it out into a sheet of dough 1 cm high. Cut out some nice biscuits and bake them in a hot oven at 200 ° for 15-18 minutes. "Angels do not see if we are beautiful or ugly, educated or illiterate, rich or poor, they only recognize the light that shines in us, they approach it to communicate with our heart.

CHAPTER 4

LUNCH RECIPE

1. Ragu Of Lentils

This legume, which does not need to be soaked, cooks in a half an hour (for peeled lentils even much less... about 10 minutes), has a gentle granulometry that is neither too large nor too small, gives consistency and a flavor that adapts beautifully to fried and tomato puree. For the white ragù (without tomato) I continue to prefer the soya okara.

Ingredients for about 4-6 people

- 1 large onion
- 1 large carrot
- 2 cloves of garlic
- 1 small celery stalk
- 1 small bowl of dried lentils (preferably small)
- half a glass of red wine
- 1 glass of tomato puree or 2 glasses of tomatoes in small pieces
- salt, pepper, desired spices (for me a classic is mace, chili pepper, and rosemary)
- extra virgin olive oil
- red wine (about half a glass)

Procedure:

a. Pour a drop of oil into a frying pan and brown over medium heat a chopped onion, garlic, carrot, and celery (more or less thin according to taste). Fry for a few minutes (for those who are against oil during cooking, you can always use simple water and use the oil at the end of cooking directly before serving the pasta), add the lentils, and let them mix. Pour the wine and let it evaporate almost completely.

b. Now we just have to add the pulp or fresh tomato, salt, pepper, chili pepper, mace, and a sprig of rosemary that we will remove at the end of cooking. Stir for a moment, pour in some water if necessary to cover the lentils, lower the heat to a minimum and place the lid on the pan. Now it will have to cook for about twenty minutes, but every now

and then let's take a look that the sauce remains quite moist. Add salt, pepper, and whatever else we like.
   c. If you have enough time I recommend preparing it in advance and letting it rest, the flavors will be much more vivid.

2. Pasta With Purple Cabbage Pesto

Ingredients:
- 9 oz of cabbage
- 3 oz of almonds
- 2 oz of pine nuts
- 1 teaspoon chopped rosemary
- 3½ oz of olive oil
- 2 tablespoons of lemon juice
- 2 oz of wholemeal bread
- 2 tablespoons of baking powder
- salt and pepper
- 1 clove of garlic

Procedure:
   a. Toast the pine nuts in a pan, remove the outer leaves of the cabbage and cut it into strips. Blend the almonds and pine nuts, then add the previously cut cabbage, add the rosemary, salt, pepper, baking powder, lemon juice and oil. Add 70 ml of water if too thick. Cut the bread into cubes and blend it, to obtain a coarse crumb. Take a pan, put 2 tablespoons of olive oil and a clove of garlic. Add the crumb and let it toast until it is golden and crispy. Cook the spaghetti in salted water. As soon as they are cooked, season with the pesto. To finish, garnish the dish with the crumb.

3. Pasta With Flowers And Herbs

Ingredients:
- oil evo
- garlic
- fresh parsley
- Fresh lemon balm
- Rosemary flowers
- Borage flowers
- flowers of Satureja
- Trassacus flowers
- saffron pistils
- Sichuan pepper
- arugula
- Sayve walnut cheese
- organic lemon peel
- fresh ginger

Procedure:

a. First of all prepare the pasta by mixing all the ingredients and working it well and then let it rest for 30 minutes covered or in a bag. Cut some pieces and roll out some snakes. From these snakes obtained with a knife small amounts of pasta and pass them to the dumplings, it is also done before and the pasta retains the sauce better.

b. Then in a pan pour oil, garlic, fresh ginger and some pistils of saffron. Start to fry gently and then fade with a little water. In this way, the saffron colours the sauce in the best possible way. Scrub over the organic lemon peel. In a mortar, crush some Sichuan peppercorns and add to the sauce. Boil the strozzapreti, drain and put in the pan with the dressing. Saute the pasta in the sauce, add parsley, rocket and flowers. Salt all the ingredients again, serve and sprinkle with a few more flowers and a few flakes of Sayve. Very good, tasty, aromatic, fragrant ... spring.

4. Apple Dumplings

Ingredients for the filling (to be made the night before):
- 2 reinette apples (or Golden)
- 1/2 golden onion, finely sliced
- salt
- 1 tuft of rosemary
- 1 tablespoon evo oil
- 3 tablespoons of VeganOK bread crumbs
- 3 tablespoons of hazelnut flour
- 1 pinch of nutmeg
- very little water

Procedure:

a. Peel the apples and cut them into not too thin slices, then fry them in a fried onion browned in olive oil, flavoring with the tuft of rosemary. Just salt and let the apples stew as if they were potatoes, then let them cool completely, before crushing them with a fork, in a boule, adding, in that order, the hazelnut flour, a little 'salt, nutmeg, breadcrumbs and a little water, just to compact the dough. Work it well and, when it is moist and firm, wrap it in a sheet of food film and let it rest in the refrigerator for one night.

Ingredients for the pasta:
- 1 cup of flour T2
- 1 pinch of turmeric powder
- Water qb

Procedure:

a. In a tureen mix the flour to which you have added the turmeric, adding as much warm water as necessary to obtain a firm and not sticky dough. Roll it out onto the pastry board with a rolling pin into 2 rectangular sheets and place piles of filling the size of a hazelnut on top of one of the sheets before overlapping the other sheet. Gently crush the dough around the filling to remove the air, then cut out some ravioli using the mold or a glass upside down. Cook the apple ravioli in a large pot of salted water and season with oil and sage, sprinkling with hazelnut flour or slightly toasted breadcrumbs. Serve hot.

CHAPTER 5

RECIPES FOR MAIN COURSES AND SINGLE DISHES

1. Aubergines Meatballs

Recipe with soya okara to add, because anyone who makes milk (or drink you want to say) knows very well what volume of "waste" (which is a resource!) is found.

Let's prepare some meatballs with a Mediterranean taste, excellent to serve with tomato sauce.

Ingredients:
- 3½-5 1/3 oz of soya okara
- 2 small aubergines
- 1 clove of garlic
- 1 tablespoon of soy sauce
- Salt and spices at will (tip oregano, garlic powder, chilli)
- 2 tablespoons of tomato pulp
- Breadcrumbs or chickpea flour or oatmeal

Procedure:
a. Fry the aubergines in chunks in a pan with a drop of water and a pinch of salt. Lower the heat and put the lid on so they cook evenly, just a few minutes. Or you can also grill.
b. Once cooked and well-dried, blend coarsely (i.e. with a mixer just give a few taps without creating a uniform puree, we want consistency!), add the spices, soy sauce, tomato, chopped garlic and okara. Mix well and gradually add a little bit of breadcrumbs or chickpea flour or oatmeal to make the dough compact (but not too much) and manipulable.
c. Form the meatballs and bake at 200 °c ventilated mode for 10-15 minutes.
d. Excellent both hot, warm and cold.

2. Tofu With Pizzaiola Sauce

Ingredients (they will be to taste, as far as the quantities are concerned)

- Two blocks of tofu (I use sojasun)
- red onion
- fresh and dry oregano
- fresh basil
- sweet paprika
- pepper
- fresh or dry garlic powder
- tomato puree (I use black moose)
- tamari sauce (not skimped)

Procedure:

a. Marinate the tofu at least half an hour with the tamari, dried or fresh garlic, paprika.

b. Fry the onion in a little oil, pour the tofu with the sauce of the marinade, brown well, at least five / seven minutes, add the tomato sauce, put salt if the tamari was not tasty enough, add fresh basil and oregano, put a little water, and cover ... let cook twenty minutes ... taste, and serve!

3. Vegatorella

Ingredients:

- Servings for 5/6 servings
- 9 oz of natural Tempeh
- 9 oz of natural Seitan
- 14 oz of natural Tofu

Spices and other powders:

- dry garlic powder
- nutmeg
- turmeric
- pepper
- cloves
- dry ginger,
- fennel seed powder
- Moringa Oleifera and/or Spirulina
- chili
- salt.

You smell:

- Bay leaves
- Sage leaves
- rosemary twigs
- twigs of thyme
- 2 red onions

Liquids:
- Vegetable stock with ¼ vegetable stock cubes, 2 carrots and half a red onion;
- a small glass of olive oil
- two glasses of non-acidulous red wine better dry sweet
- a glass of Nocino walnut-husk liqueur
- a glass of balsamic vinegar
- a glass of apple vinegar.

Sweeteners:
- 2 tablespoons of malted rice or barley
- 2 teaspoons of whole cane sugar
- 1 apple or 1 pear.

Procedure:
 a. Prepare INFUSE with about : 400 cc vegetable stock prepared with 2 carrots, Carum Carvi cumin seeds (not the classic cumin, they have different flavors), ¼ organic vegetable stock cube, half red onion, three cloves, slices of apple or pear, 2 teaspoons of brown sugar whole.
 b. In the meantime, in another container, put finely sliced red onion, fresh bay leaves, sage leaves, rosemary twigs, thyme twigs, a small glass of olive oil, two glasses of non-acidic Red Wine, with a dry sweet taste, a small glass of Nocino liqueur from walnut husk, a small glass of balsamic vinegar, a small glass of apple vinegar, two spoonfuls of rice or barley malt, a sprinkling of: dry garlic powder, nutmeg, dry ginger (so that you feel little), turmeric, pepper.
 c. Optional: a spoon of Moringa Oleifera (used as a supplement powder or even a teaspoon of spirulina powder) contributing to the color and flavor of the wild and enriching the nutritional content of the preparation.
 d. Other spices and smells at will such as a few finely ground fennel seeds, or spices a little 'spicy depending on taste (the chili will then put in the final passage in the pan...).
 e. Add the filtered vegetable broth to the preparation, add a little salt, mix and leave to infuse for at least 4 hours, but also more.
 f. After a while, put the whole infusion back into a small pot and boil for a few minutes to allow the alcohol to evaporate.
 g. In the meantime, cut Seitan, Tofu and Tempeh into small pieces that are more irregular and can even be broken up with your hands (it should not be diced but have a "natural" effect).
 h. Put all the pieces back into a large, low container, and cover with the lukewarm infusion, and from there, stirring occasionally, even every few minutes.
 i. 4 hours, leave to infuse even for 24 hours or more without any problems in the refrigerator.

j. When it is time to serve the Veggoratella: put olive oil in a pan, add a little 'of chilli depending on taste, and put the pieces of mixed Veggoratella drained from the liquid (the onion is already included and already marinated so it will be all very digestible, but if you want you can add at the moment more onion and even a clove of garlic then remove) and sauté a little', and adjust salt.

4. Seitan Greenery

Ingredients:

- 4 slices of grilled seitan (about 50 g each)
- 7 oz Brussels sprouts
- 7 oz of pumpkin
- 1 organic red apple
- For marinating
- 3 oz of maple syrup
- 1+ 1/2 teaspoon mustard
- 1 teaspoon of fresh or dried thyme
- 1 teaspoon of olive oil
- a pinch of garlic powder

Procedure:

a. To start, prepare the marinade, combining the ingredients and stirring well.
b. Transfer the marinade to a container or food bag such as those for freezing, preferably with the zip closure.
c. Place the seitan in the marinade and massage it so that the marinade covers all the slices. If you use the food bag, close it and perform the operation from the outside.
d. Let it rest in the fridge for at least two hours.
e. During the rest of the seitan, you can take care of the vegetables.
f. Wash and clean the Brussels sprouts, cut them in half and set aside.
g. Peel the pumpkin and cut it into cubes. Put it aside, too, together with the cabbage.
h. Finally, cut the apple into cubes, without peeling, and add it to the vegetables.
i. Dress the vegetables with two tablespoons of extra virgin olive oil, salt and pepper to taste.
j. Turn on the static oven and bring it to 200°.
k. Oil the base of a baking sheet or cover it with baking paper and put the vegetables back in place, trying to distribute them well in the baking sheet.
l. Bake for about 20 minutes, then remove the pan from the oven and create a space in the center between the vegetables, in which you will store the marinated seitan.

5. Tempeh Leek And Pepper

Ingredients:

- A tempeh bale (usually 250 g pack)
- a leek
- a red pepper
- soy sauce or tamari
- sweet paprika
- self-produced balsamic vinegar
- evo oil

Preparation:

a. Slice the tempeh bread into slices, but if you like also squares like stew will do very well. Then prepare a marinade of dark soya, sweet paprika and balsamic vinegar in which you will dip the tempeh and let it rest as much as possible. I kept it in a bowl covered with transparent film in the refrigerator all night long. Cut the leek into slices and the pepper into strips and let them wilt in a pan with a drizzle of olive oil, add the tempeh and cook over medium heat. You can accompany it with basmati rice if necessary and you will have a single dish complete with proteins and carbohydrates.

6. Tofu With Shoots

Ingredients:

- two carrots
- a zucchini
- a dozen or so cherry tomatoes.
- 6 oz of bamboo shoots
- two tofu blocks (about 250 g)
- rice oil
- black pepper
- soy sauce
- curry
- ginger powder
- hot pepper

Preparation:

a. I cut the tofu into cubes and put it to marinate with spices and soy sauce in the refrigerator for a few hours. I drained the bamboo shoots and rinsed them under running water and meanwhile I cut the vegetables and sautéed them in a non-stick pan with a drizzle of rice oil. I then added the tofu and the sprouts and cooked them over a high flame until cooked. If necessary add water if you see that it dries too much.

b. The longer the tofu remains to marinate, the more it acquires flavour. I personally left it for half a day in the fridge, so much so that the soy sauce had been completely absorbed by the tofu after the time. I recommend not adding salt to the preparation.

7. Seitan In Spicy Sauce

Ingredients:

- 4 thick slices of seitan
- Worcestershire Sauce
- soy sauce
- habanero sauce
- spicy paprika and sweet paprika
- sesame seeds

Procedure:

a. I cut the slices of seitan into cubes and marinated them in a bowl together with the sauces mixed together and the paprika. Of course, the longer the marinating time, the more the seitan will taste.

b. After the marinating time I heated up a non-stick pan and toasted a handful of sesame seeds lightly.

c. I poured the seitan morsels, turning them immediately so that the sesame adheres to all the cubes, and over a high heat I blew it all up.

8. Farifrittata

Ingredients:

- a generous tip of chopped rocket,
- a few leaves of sage,
- half an onion, finely chopped,
- chickpea flour,
- red lentil flour,
- pink salt,
- turmeric,
- ginger,
- nettle powder (dried nettles),
- I'm just gonna get you enough water,
- little oil for cooking

Preparation:

a. Mix the flours in the water in the desired quantity to obtain a semi-dense batter, add the spices as desired, meanwhile, fry the herbs and onion in a non-stick pan. When the onion is withered, cover with the batter, cook over a low heat until it becomes firm, then turn it over and cook on the other side for a few minutes. You can vary with flours using flours from different legumes that with herbs, I use rocket, ribs, radish leaves, turnip leaves, dandelion, all great!

9. Almonds And Carrots Patties

Ingredients:

- 2 lbs of carrots
- 3 oz of peeled almonds
- halls

- 1 tablespoon EVO oil.

Procedure:

a. Extract the juice from the carrots and drink it as an appetizer. Then mix the carrot pulp with the almonds reduced to flour, oil and salt. Shape the meatballs and dish them: I used them as a second side dish for red asparagus rice and accompanied them with a guacamole of avocado and raw asparagus.

10. Curry Soya Stew

Ingredients:

- 5 1/3 oz of soya stew to be rehydrated
- 2 zucchini cut into pieces
- 2 eggplants cut into small pieces
- 4 tablespoons of Evo oil
- 1 clove of garlic, chopped
- 5 ladles of vegetable broth
- 7 oz of self-produced soya cream
- 2 teaspoons of curry
- 1 chopped chilli pepper
- salt
- 1 pinch of turmeric
- 15 self-produced pitted olives

Procedure:

a. Put the pieces of soya into boiling water for 15 minutes. Put the oil, garlic and vegetables in a non-stick pan and brown them well, then add the drained and squeezed pieces of soya, let them gain flavour, add the olives, turmeric and chilli pepper and cook for about 20 minutes, adding the broth when necessary; 5 minutes before the end of cooking add the curry, cream and salt.

11. Seitan Medallions

Ingredients:

- 4 thick slices of seitan
- 18 oz of mushrooms
- 1 oz of dried mushrooms
- 3½ oz of bamboo shoots
- 1 handful of parsley
- potato starch
- vegetable broth
- evo oil
- salt, pepper

Procedure:

a. Soak the dried mushrooms in lukewarm water for the time necessary to rehydrate them. Clean the mushrooms and slice them thinly. Heat some Evo oil in a non-stick pan and add all the mushrooms. In the meantime, put the seitan slices in the potato starch. Cook the mushrooms for 15-20 minutes. If necessary, add some vegetable broth. Add the "floured" seitan and the bamboo shoots and finish cooking for another 15 minutes. Also in this step, if necessary, soak with the broth. Finely chop the parsley and add it when cooked, adding salt and pepper. Serve with polenta, mashed potatoes or steamed potatoes. For a stronger flavour you can add a clove of garlic during cooking. For a very strong flavor you can chop, with parsley, raw garlic.

The point:
a. I try as much as possible to buy food at kilometer zero or almost. Bamboo shoots certainly do not fall into this category and, perhaps, are not even a very ethical food, thinking of the extinction of pandas. But every now and then I believe that it is necessary to support the economy of some countries and, above all, not to deny oneself the experience of tasting food from other cultures because, as I often say, cooking is a bridge between peoples.

12. Soya Escalope

Ingredients:

- 11 oz of seitan
- 2 carrots
- 11 oz of date tomatoes
- 1 onion
- 1/2 glass of white wine
- 2 tablespoons of taggiasca olives
- 1 tablespoon chopped parsley
- 2 tablespoons of soy sauce
- flour
- evo oil
- halls
- 1 teaspoon of granular vegetable cube

Procedure:
a. Cut the seitan into thin slices, flour it and fry it in hot evo oil, remove the slices from the pan and place them on a sheet of fried paper and, in the remaining oil, fry the chopped onion. When the onion takes on colour, add the diced carrots, salt and cook for 10 minutes on a low heat. Add the seitan, raise the heat and add the white wine, fade; now add 1 glass of lukewarm water, the granulated vegetable stock cube, the tomatoes cut in half, the soy sauce and the olives. Leave to cook until the sauce has thickened, about 30 minutes. Garnish with chopped parsley.

13. Zucchini And Tofu Skewers

Ingredients:

- 4 zucchini

- 2 tofu blocks
- parsley
- garlic
- evo oil
- halls

Procedure:
   a. Boil the tofu for about 10 minutes. Cut it into small squares and leave it to gain flavor for 2 hours in a marinade of oil, salt, parsley and finely chopped garlic. Clean the courgettes and cut them into slices about 2 cm thick. Boil the pieces for about 10 minutes keeping them as firm as possible. Thread in, alternating pieces of courgettes and pieces of tofu and put them to brown on a hot plate for another 10-15 minutes turning them on all sides. When golden, brush with a little olive oil, salt if necessary and serve.

The point
   a. The skewers can be served with aromatic rice balls (soon the recipe) and a simple soianese made with soy yogurt, salt and sweet mustard emulsified together.

14. Breaded Slices Of Seitan

Ingredients (for 2 people):
- 14 oz of grilled seitan
- 3 oz of wholemeal breadcrumbs
- 3 oz of chickpea flour
- 4 tablespoons of shoyu sauce
- 4 tablespoons of Evo oil
- water qb

Procedure:
   a. On a plate, prepare the breadcrumbs by adding a little shoyu sauce and olive oil. Shell well with a fork and add a drop of water if necessary. On another plate, prepare the batter with chickpea flour and water. Pass the slices of seitan (in my case there were 4) first in the chickpea batter then in the breadcrumbs. Put them in a non-stick pan and brown them well on both sides. It won't take long to cook them and you'll be able to adjust them easily. When the seitan is ready, place it on your plate and accompany it with the vegetables of your choice.

15. Happy Chicken Tempeh

Ingredients:
- 7 oz tempeh
- juice of 2-3 oranges
- ¾ oz of flour T2
- 1 oz almonds
- 1/3 oz sesame seeds

- 2 teaspoons of sweet paprika
- 1 tablespoon low evo oil
- nutmeg qb
- pepper
- salt at will
- water qb

Procedure:

a. Nothing could be simpler! In a small bowl, cut the almonds into not too small pieces (I used a mortar), add the sesame seeds, flour and spices except the paprika. Also add salt if you like. Cut the tempeh into pieces and throw it into the bowl, stir well so that the flour adheres to all pieces. In another bowl squeeze the juice of the oranges and stretch it with 1-2 tablespoons of water. At this point in a non-stick pan start to brown the tempeh, if the oil dries just add 2 tablespoons of water, I to adjust with the cooking time I put the water twice and when it dries completely to all the orange juice. Then season with paprika and let it dry on a moderate flame: it must remain a little 'of orange sauce, so I recommend not to make it stand too much on the fire.

16. Spicy Tofu With Cauliflower

Ingredients:

- 2 tofu rolls (250 g in all)
- 4-5 rosettes of cooked cauliflower (I have plenty)
- paprika
- pepper
- curry
- tamari sauce
- vegetable oil
- parsley
- 1 clove of garlic
- sesame seeds

Procedure:

a. Start by squeezing the tofu between your hands and cutting it into cubes; put them in a bowl to marinate together with 2 tablespoons of tamari (also here go according to your taste), a pinch of paprika (I like spicy), plenty of curry, pepper, a sprig of chopped parsley, a sprinkling of sesame seeds and chopped garlic clove. Put in the fridge and let it rest (the more it rests the more tasty it will be). Put a drop of oil in a pan and brown the tofu. Then add the cauliflower florets in pieces and cook for about 15 minutes until everything is well amalgamated and flavored (if it dries too much add a drop of water) Adjust the tamarisk or spices and serve sprinkling with smoked paprika if you like.

17. Seitan Tonnato

Ingredients:

- 7 oz of self-produced seitan cut thinly
- 2 tablespoons salted capers
- 1 glass of apple vinegar
- 7 oz of soya mayonnaise with self-produced mustard
- 1 tablespoon vegetable cube
- 1 teaspoon xanthan mix
- 1 teaspoon garlic powder

Procedure:

a. Put the washed capers in a glass of vinegar and leave them to soak for 30 minutes. Set aside some capers, the others squeeze and blend with mayonnaise, stock cube, xanthan mix. Put a little cream on the plate then place the slices of seitan and cover with the rest of the cream; put some slices of lemon and some capers to decorate, cover with film and refrigerate until it is time to serve. It must rest for at least 2 hours.

18. Mopur

Ingredients:

- 2 slices of steak/mopur fillet meal
- evo oil
- 1/2 orange juice filtered
- 1/2 lemon juice filtered
- 1/2 glass of white wine
- halls

Procedure:

a. Flour the slices of mopur and place them in a non-stick pan with very little oil to brown for 2 minutes on both sides. Wet them with white wine and when the alcohol has evaporated add the juice of the citrus fruits. Cook with the lid for another 3-4 minutes and serve.

19. Pumpkin Soya Stew

Ingredients:

- 3½ oz of soya morsels
- 2 lbs pumpkin
- Shoyu sauce
- curry
- paprika
- vegetable broth (which you can make with granular if you don't have time, the important thing is that it doesn't contain glutamate)
- 1 red onion

Procedure:

a. First of all cut the pumpkin into cubes (I like to leave the peel, of course after washing it carefully, because it becomes nice tender cooking, but you can peel it) and steam it for 20 minutes, until it is nice tender.

b. Then rehydrate the soy chunks: bring the vegetable stock to the boil (you will need at least 1 litre of it) then add the soy chunks and turn off the heat. Leave to rest for 10 minutes, then drain and squeeze them well in a sieve, so that all the excess water comes out. Put the chopped onion in a large frying pan, add the pumpkin and leave to gain flavor for 5 minutes. Then add the rehydrated stew, blend with 2-3 tablespoons of shoyu and cook for 20 minutes, adding some vegetable broth if it dries too much. Finally, add curry and spicy paprika, then serve?

20. Polpettone

Ingredients:
- 4 oz of okara
- 1¾ oz of soya bulgur
- 1 carrot
- 1 onion
- 1 clove of garlic
- 1 tablespoon desalted capers
- thyme
- chives
- basil
- salt (or self-produced nut)
- 2-3 tablespoons starch (or starch)
- 2 tablespoons of tamarisk
- 2 tablespoons of Evo oil

Procedure:
a. Toast the bulgur in a pan after rinsing it, add twice the volume of broth and let it cook for a few minutes, it should remain al dente because it will continue to cook in the oven! Trim vegetables, capers and herbs finely and mix them with okara together with oil and tamari. We also incorporate the bulgur that has absorbed all the broth and starch.

21. Soia

Ingredients (for 2-3 people):
- 3½ oz of soybean steaks (also the morsels are good)
- 7 oz Piccadilly tomatoes (or cherries, or you do it!)
- 1 tablespoon of olive oil
- 1 piece of onion (qui de gustibus?)
- chilli
- rosemary
- halls

Procedure:
a. Brown the onion, cut into not too small cubes, in the oil; add the cherry tomatoes cut in half, rosemary, salt and chilli pepper. Let the

sauce thicken well. At this point add the soybean steaks (previously rehydrated in boiling water for 10 minutes, cooled and squeezed well).

22. Wheat Muscle In Stew

Ingredients (for 3 people):

- 6 oz of chickpea flour
- 4 oz of rice flour
- 2 oz of corn flour
- 3 cups of tomato paste
- 5 cups of tamari sauce
- ¾ cup of water
- salt

Procedure:

a. Add all the ingredients and mix well until you get a soft and sticky mixture, place it on wet baking paper, roll it up like a salami and tie the sides with string.
b. Place in a preheated oven at 180° for 1/2 hour. At this point it is ready to be cooked to your liking. I decided to make the stew, I prepared a red sauce rich in vegetables (carrots, celery) with a pinch of chili, towards the end of cooking I added the muscle of wheat cubes and I did flavor.
c. Accompanied by crispy baked potatoes.

23. Soya And Eggplant Morsels

Ingredients:

- 3½ oz of dehydrated soya morsels
- 1 large eggplant
- 1/4 blond onion
- 1 cup of pine nuts
- 1 cup of raisins
- 4 basil leaves
- 2 cups apple vinegar
- 2 cups cane sugar
- 2 cups shoyu (soy sauce)
- oil evo qb
- salt
- glaze of balsamic vinegar (to decorate)

Procedure:

a. Soak the soya morsels in boiling broth according to the instructions in the package, then drain them and let them cool. At this point squeeze them out to release as much water as possible and quickly pass them in a non-stick pan so that they brown slightly, when they take color, wet them with the soy sauce and remove them from the heat. In the same pan, add a little oil and - when it is hot - add the finely chopped onion and diced eggplant. Cook over a lively flame for about 10' turning often and finally add the soya morsels, pine nuts, raisins (previously soaked in a little warm water), a pinch of salt and sugar stirring well to mix. At this point add the vinegar and let it flavour until the steam that rises from the pan has lost the pungent and alcoholic tone of the vinegar, it will take 1 minute, continue to turn. Add the basil again in pieces and put on a plate, garnishing with balsamic vinegar icing. Enjoy your meal!

Considerations:
- a. It's a "second course" with a strong flavour, which plays on the sweet-and-sour encounter, so it goes well with side dishes that favour the sweet (such as carrot salad with grapes) or equally defined (such as friggitelli with tomato sauce).

24. Slap In The Face

Ingredients:
- sliced wholemeal rye bread
- 1 glass of chickpea flour
- water qb
- 1 clove of red garlic
- cornmeal to taste
- 1 pinch of nutmeg
- corn seed oil (for frying)
- fresh sage leaves
- dried sage powder
- mint leaves
- salt, pepper to taste

Procedure:
- a. Add a pinch of salt, pepper and enough water to the chickpea flour to form a semi-liquid batter, which we leave to rest in the fridge for 2 hours. After this time, rub the slices of rye bread with the clove of garlic and the leaves of fresh sage, which we will first pass in the batter, then in corn flour mixed with cinnamon and a pinch of sage powder.
- b. Fry our cutlets in boiling oil until they are golden and then lay them on absorbent kitchen paper before serving them very hot, sprinkled with salt and leaves of mint and sage on a bed of salad.

25. Chickpeas And Spinach With Andalusian Sauce

Ingredients for 3 people:
- 2 lbs of fresh spinach
- 12½ oz of chickpeas (drained)
- 2 tablespoons of tomato puree
- 2 cloves of garlic
- 1/3 teaspoon of cumin
- 1/3 teaspoon of paprika

- a pinch of black pepper
- EVO oil q.b

Procedure:

a. The day before I slowly cooked the chickpeas (after soaking them overnight) and finally I added (very little) salt. While I washed the spinach carefully, removing the larger stems, I did not drain them perfectly and I stewed them in their water. Once cooked, I let them cool down and chopped them roughly.

b. Cut spinach, proceed with the fried. Here I show you the spices I used, the pimentòn is Spanish, here you use a lot, but I think it is equivalent to paprika, as the label suggests. The original recipe, illustrated to me by my grandmothers anadaluse, includes five cloves of garlic! In order not to compromise my social life and that of my guests, I used one, but you are free to follow the original recipe.

c. Once the garlic has been cut into slices, sauté gently with the spices until golden brown.

d. Add the drained spinach to the sautéed mixture, keeping aside the little cooking water left over from the stew, and let it be flavoured with oil and spices. After a few minutes add the chickpeas and turn to absorb the scents. Cover with vegetable broth, color with two tablespoons of tomato sauce and leave to simmer for half an hour with the lid. After 30 minutes, remove the lid and leave to dry: the mixture must be fairly dry, must not have the consistency of a soup.

e. Serve with ground black pepper.

26. Chickpea Meatballs And Yoghurt Sauce

Ingredients:

- 2 potatoes
- 1 box of cooked chickpeas
- 2 cloves of garlic
- herbal salt
- breadcrumbs
- chickpea flour
- 1 jar of soya yoghurt
- evo oil
- the juice of 1 lemon
- parsley

Procedure:

a. Boil the potatoes and mash them with a fork. Chop the chickpeas and add them to the mashed potatoes. Put everything in a bowl together with a clove of chopped garlic and add the breadcrumbs and a nice pinch of salt flavoured with herbs.

b. Make balls of it and roll them in the chickpea flour. Finally bake at 180° for about 20 minutes.

c. In the meantime, prepare the yoghurt sauce by combining the yoghurt with a drizzle of olive oil, the juice of a lemon, 1 clove of garlic finely chopped and decorating with a leaf of parsley.

27. Burger Pumpinks

Ingredients:
- 1 burger sandwich
- 18 oz of pumpkin
- 1 potato
- evo oil
- 1 tablespoon of soy sauce
- 1 clove of garlic
- breadcrumbs to taste
- leaves of mâche to decorate
- 1 onion
- 1 tablespoon of balsamic vinegar cream

Procedure:
a. Slice the pumpkin, peel the potato and put it, diced, in a pot with a drizzle of olive oil. Add the spoonful of soy sauce.
b. Cook for about 30 minutes, however, until the potato and pumpkin become "cream".
c. I only crushed them with a fork. Coldly add the sliced garlic and breadcrumbs and make 4 burgers.
d. Line a baking sheet with baking paper and bake in a hot oven at 220° for about 30 minutes.
e. Once golden, cut the sandwich and put in a pumpkin burger. In the meantime, fry a sliced onion in a little olive oil, add the tablespoon of balsamic vinegar.
f. Finally fill the sandwich with onion, salad leaves and ... enjoy. I did not put any further sauce because in my opinion it was already so tasty and in my opinion vegan mayonnaise or ketchup would spoil the taste.

28. Rye And Wholemeal Oats With Garden Flowers

Ingredients:
- Ecor wholemeal rye
- Wholemeal oats Ecor
- fresh onion
- leek
- evo oil
- Fresh tarragon
- Satureja
- zucchini flowers and pumpkins
- Nasturtium Flowers
- yellow zucchini
- halls

- fresh chilli
- lemon peel
- grains of pistachio

Procedure:

a. The evening before soak the cereals - 12 hours. Day after cook them for 45 minutes. In a pan put oil, fresh onion, leek, satureja, tarragon, lemon peel and chilli. Start to fry gently. After cooking the cereals add them to the pan, add the zucchini and flowers and sauté over a high flame. Sprinkle with pistachio grains.

29. Chickpeas, Cauliflowers, Tamari And Yoghurt Sauce

Ingredients for cauliflowers:

- Cauliflowers
- black sesame
- curry
- turmeric
- black pepper
- dry garlic
- halls

For the sauce:

- 9 oz of Soya yoghurt
- biodynamic half lemon juice
- tahina or tahin, two teaspoons
- halls
- parsley qb

For the chickpeas:

- Boiled chickpeas
- diced onion
- Tamari ... as much as you want... for me as if there were no tomorrow
- rosemary
- black pepper
- dry garlic

Procedure:

a. Take the steamed cauliflowers, cut them into small pieces, keep them aside. Put a drop of oil in a pan, brown the curry, turmeric, black pepper. add the cauliflowers...add salt...stir-fry for five minutes...and sprinkle with black sesame. For the sauce, simply...mix everything together and be generous with the poor cauliflowers:)

b. For the chickpeas... fry the onion, add the chickpeas, pepper, dried garlic...rosemary. Put the tamari, salt and let go on a moderate heat ten minutes ... compose your wonderful dish ... close your eyes, and enjoy with pleasure!

30. Millet And Red Turnips

Ingredients:

- millet
- red turnip
- garlic
- Ecor organic corn
- Umeboshi Acidulate
- evo oil
- black and white sesame seeds
- fresh chilli
- chives
- halls

Procedure:

a. Cook the millet (7 oz of millet and 18 oz of water) under the lid until the water is completely absorbed. While the millet is cooking, put the oil, coarsely grated turnip, fresh chilli pepper, sesame seeds and chopped garlic in a pan. Fry lightly, add water - not too much, acidulated Umeboshi and cook until the turnip becomes tender, towards the end of cooking add corn and cook until the liquid is absorbed. When millet is cooked, you will see that it is sticky, do not panic, it's fine! Now, season with turnip and corn.

b. Mix well until it becomes nice red. Put a little oil in the pan, add the millet and start to fry it by shelling it as you do with couscous. When you see that it is soft, shelled add sprinkle with fresh chives and serve.

31. Triangles Delight

Ingredients:

For the pasta:

- 9 oz of semolina flour
- A pinch of salt
- 1 tablespoon evo oil
- Water enough

For the seasoning :

- 14 oz of cooked chickpeas
- 2 dried tomatoes in pieces
- 3 tablespoons of Evo oil
- 1 peeled whole garlic
- 1 teaspoon of cumin powder
- 1 chilli pepper in small pieces
- 1 tablespoon of tomato sauce
- 1 tablespoon chopped parsley
- Salt to taste
- 1 glass of water
- 1 handful of flakes of food-grade yeast

Procedure:

a. In a bowl put the semolina, salt and mix, add, the oil, water and knead until you get a soft and elastic dough, cover it and let it rest for half an hour. In a non-stick pan put the oil evo, with the whole garlic and brown for a few minutes, add the chickpeas, chili pepper, dried tomatoes, let flavor for a few minutes. Add cumin, salt, tomato sauce, a glass of water, cook for 10 minutes. Take the dough, flour the pastry board, spread with your hands not too thin, cut into strips then into rectangles.

b. In a pot bring to the boil abundant salted water, cook the rectangles for 5 or 6 minutes. Drain and add them in a pan with the sauce, adding 3 ladles of cooking water, thicken for a few minutes then turn off and sprinkle with parsley. Plant and sprinkle with yeast.

32. Sorghum And Lentils

Ingredients for 2 portions:

- 3 oz sorghum (raw)
- 1 box of cooked red lentils
- 1/2 (half) celery stalk
- 1 small carrot
- 2 onions
- garlic powder a pinch
- 1¾ oz of grated large smoked tofu
- 5-6 cherry tomatoes
- salt
- evo
- lemon juice (one splash)
- balsamic vinegar
- soy sauce

Procedure:

a. Soak sorghum X for the time you find recommended on the package. Wash the vegetables and lentils and put them to drain clean onions and cut them into rather large washers, put on the stove a pot with water X the sorghum. Put on the fire a pan with its own a drizzle of oil and pour into the onions cut into rounds and let brown, when they are just golden, pour a splash of balsamic vinegar, let the cork dry and remove from the heat. Set aside. In the same pan pour a little more oil, the carrot and celery cut into small cubes, with a little onion and a pinch of garlic powder, when the celery and carrot are still crisp, pour us on a spray of soy sauce, keep the heat medium low to avoid burning the vegetables, soy sauce dried and now it's the turn of the lentils that you let drain before. Down in the pot, cook slowly, if you see that it is too small, adjust with very little water and continue cooking gently. Now it's the turn of the tomatoes, cut them in half, place them on an oiled baking sheet or on baking paper and now, inside the heat until they look nice cooked, do not put salt or sugar, these are not confit but simply and naturally baked in the oven. When they are ready, remove them from the oven and let them rest. As for the cooking time, here I have to apologize because I do not know, I only have a microwave that also acts as a ventilated oven, so you have to adjust the cooking according to your type of oven. Does the water boil? Then throw in the sorghum and let it boil for the recommended time always on the package or cook it of the consistency you prefer. I don't really like al dente but very well cooked at what point is the lentil sauce? Does it look good to you? Season with salt but it won't be necessary, soya has already thought of it, a light splash of lemon mixed well. Cook the sorghum and drain it, and it's time to create our autumn dish and comforting, with warm and enveloping scents. If you want to arzigogolararvi life, take a cup of pasta and thus create the layers a layer of sauce lentils, a layer of sorghum, a layer of smoked tofu, here, are you park ok? The tofu has an intense flavor and we do not want it to overpower the flavor of the lentils, so finish composing your little tower on top put the tomatoes and onion rings, a thread of evo done.

33. Bean Meatballs

Ingredients for 2 people:

- 5 oz of pre-cooked beans Bio
- 3½ oz of Tofu
- ½ Red onion
- 1 pinch of Curry
- Fennel seeds to taste
- Parsley to taste
- Salt to taste
- Wholemeal breadcrumbs to taste
- Corn flour to taste
- Evo oil to taste

Procedure:

a. In a kitchen mixer, blend the beans with tofu, coarsely chopped onion, curry, fennel seeds, a handful of parsley and salt to taste to form a smooth and homogeneous mixture. Add the breadcrumbs sparingly and blend to mix evenly, until they reach a dense and compact consistency, which can be easily shaped. Shape the balls of medium size with your hands and pass them in the corn flour. Cook them in a pan with a drizzle of oil, until golden brown. Serve hot!

34. Legume Olives

Ingredients :

- 9¾ oz boiled beans with the eye
- 8 oz of boiled chickpeas
- 1 teaspoon of cumin powder
- 1 teaspoon of fine salt
- 1/3 oz of chopped onion

- 1/3 oz of chopped parsley
- 3½ oz of soya milk
- 1 tablespoon full of evo oil
- 2 tablespoons of flour 0
- Grated bread to taste
- Oil evo q.b.

Procedure:

a. In a food processor chop the beans with the chickpeas, fine but not smoothed. Put the legumes in a bowl, add the onion, parsley, salt, cumin, mix with a wooden spoon, add the spoonful of olive oil, milk and then add the flour, if the 'dough was too soft add a little more flour, knead with your hands. With the dough form small balls like olives and pass them in the breadcrumbs. Grease a baking sheet with oil and place the "olives of legumes" in a hot oven at 200 degrees for 20 minutes.

35. Spelt And Coconut Salad

Ingredients for 2 people:
- 5 oz of coconut spelt
- 11 oz of brown mushrooms mushrooms
- 1 piece of orange pumpkin
- 2 red aubergines of Rotonda
- wild rocket
- 6 chopped walnuts
- oil evo q.b.
- pink salt to taste
- turmeric to taste for the pumpkin
- pepper
- rosemary
- oregano
- garlic

Procedure:

a. Cook the coconut spelt according to the instructions on the package, when it is cooked put it in a container and leave to cool. Clean the mushrooms, slice them and put them in a non-stick pan, turn on and cover with a lid. When they have dried, add a clove of garlic cut in half, very little olive oil, salt and pepper, and leave to gain flavor for a few minutes, turning them often. When cooked, place them on a plate. Clean the pan. Cut the pumpkin into cubes, pour them into the pan, add garlic and rosemary, a drizzle of olive oil and cook them, turning them often, before finishing cooking salt, add the turmeric and pepper.

b. Place the pumpkin on a plate near the mushrooms. Clean the pan. Clean and dice the aubergines, cook in a pan with garlic a drizzle of olive oil and a pinch of oregano, at the end of cooking add salt. Place the aubergines on a plate with other vegetables and leave to cool.

36. Bean And Rosemary Chips

Ingredients

- 2 parts Borlotti beans (I used dried ones but you can take those already cooked, the important thing is to drain them very well)
- 1 part or even a little less boiled rice of the Batter
- Rosemary - to your taste
- Garlic
- Breadcrumbs to taste
- Salt and pepper to taste

Procedure:

a. If you are using dried beans, cook them in a pressure cooker with a piece of Kombu seaweed (after soaking for at least 12 hours and changing the water). Prepare the batter now and refrigerate. Turn on the oven at 180°C. Now put the garlic and rosemary needles in a blender.

b. Chop the beans well, then put the cooked and drained beans and the boiled rice into a blender and continue to blend. Add the batter a little at a time until you obtain a homogeneous mixture, not too liquid. If necessary, add a little breadcrumbs, taste and season with salt and pepper. Cover a baking sheet with baking paper and, with the help of a spoon, pour over the dough in small portions. Keep the chips apart because they will swell during cooking. Rather, make two bakes. Let it go for 20 minutes, then turn the chips over and let it go for another 20 minutes. You can serve these chips very hot, but also at room temperature, maybe accompanied by a little 'Mayonnaise VEG.

37. Meatloaf Of Legumes

Ingredients:

- 1 cup of cooked black beans;
- 1 cup of cooked cannellini beans;
- 1/2 cup veg-giano (flaked yeast - almonds - salt - nutmeg);
- 1 cup of breadcrumbs;
- 1 clove of garlic;
- fresh chopped parsley;
- pink salt to taste
- 1 tablespoon of kuzu;
- EVO oil to taste

For cooking

- Water;
- 2 teaspoons vegetable cube
- 2 tablespoons of soy sauce
- Tuna-like sauce.

Ingredients:

- 1 cup of soy yogurt;

- 1/4 cup of EVO oil;
- 1/2 lemon juice;
- 1/2 clove of garlic ;
- a tablespoon of parsley;
- 5/6 capers;
- a teaspoon of a mixture of seaweed chopped into flour.

Procedure:
   a. Chop not too finely beans, garlic and parsley, add the breadcrumbs, veg-giano and kuzu dissolved in a little water, 2 tablespoons of oil and a pinch of salt. Kuzu is a vegetable starch and is used to thicken the dough a little.
   b. Adjust the consistency: if the dough is too soft add a little 'breadcrumbs or a tablespoon of flour, on the contrary, if it is too thick add a little' water.
   c. Knead, form a sausage and wrap with a cotton cloth tying the ends.
   d. In a large pot prepare the cooking broth with water, vegetable stock cubes and a couple of tablespoons of soy sauce. Dip the meatloaf to be covered with the broth, bring to the boil and leave to cook for 30 minutes, 15/20 minutes if you use the pressure cooker. Remove the meatloaf from the pot, let it cool down a few minutes before opening the cooking sheet to avoid scalding.
   e. Let it cool down because it cuts much better when cold. Serve in slices together with a green sauce or a sauce similar to tuna.

38. Zuppa Has Profumi Of Orientation

Ingredients for 2 people:
- 3½ oz of spelt
- 4 oz of previously cooked chickpeas
- 1 white yam
- 1 bunch of spinach
- leek
- evo oil
- halls
- pepper
- turmeric
- Garam Masala
- 1 tablespoon of dehydrated coconut

Procedure:
   a. Cook the spelt as indicated on the package. In a wok put a drizzle of oil, a sliced leek and diced batata and pepper. Let it fry and add 2 glasses of water.

39. Fonio Meatballs And Vegetables

Ingredients:
- B.M.S. Organic Cooked Fonio

- Carrots
- courgettes
- rice flour
- rice milk
- cornflour
- Yeast flakes
- halls
- of good oil evo for frying

Procedure:

a. I started cooking fonio. Bring the salted water to the boil with a drizzle of oil. The amount of water should be 2.5 - 3 times greater than the amount of fonio (a tablespoon of fonio should cook in three tablespoons of water). I poured the fonio and cooked it until it absorbed all the water. Once it was ready, I let it rest and cool in a pot with a lid on top. In the meantime I cut the courgettes into cubes and blown them up in the wok pot with a drizzle of Evo oil. Cut the carrots into julienne pieces, which I added halfway through cooking the courgettes to soften them up a bit. Once I had cooled both the fonio and the vegetables, I added them, adding the flaked yeast, salt, fresh parsley pepper and I mixed all the ingredients. I prepared some dishes, with which, in one I poured the rice flour, in another I poured the milk and another one the corn flour for the breadcrumbs. I took a small amount of fonio and worked it well to give it the shape and compact it into rather small meatballs so they don't break and are prettier. I first passed them in rice flour, then in milk and then in corn flour. I continued until I finished all the ingredients. In a pan I put a good amount of oil, I heated it up, but not too much, I let the meatballs fry three minutes from each side and I put them on absorbent paper to make them lose the excess oil, in short, normal frying process, to be done well and very rarely! Since these meatballs had a delicate taste, we ate them with a vegan mayonnaise accompanied by a fresh and light salad.

40. Hummus Black

Ingredients:

- About 4 oz of previously boiled black chickpeas
- 1 clove of garlic or granular garlic
- oil evo qb
- black pepper
- half a lemon juice
- black salt flakes
- tahina sauce one tablespoon

Procedure:

a. It's a very simple recipe. To shorten the time I cooked the chickpeas in a pressure cooker and I smoothed them with the juice of half a lemon, flakes of black salt of cypress, a clove of garlic deprived of its soul (also fine dry granular one), the tahina sauce of pepper and extra virgin olive oil. An excellent sauce that goes well with Arab bread, corn tortillas or vegetable crudités.

Considerations:
   a. Compared to common chickpeas I have noticed that they cook in a shorter time, and it is no small thing if you are in a hurry. Soaking in water is however expected before cooking. They have a more delicate flavor and are very creamy, for the sauce if I had omitted the olive oil would still have been creamy, even without the addition of liquids such as oil precisely.

41. Pumpkin And Black Cabbage Rice

Ingredients:
- 1¾ oz of brown rice
- 3½ oz of ornamental pumpkin
- 1¾ oz of black cabbage
- 1 shallot
- Evo oil qb
- Salt

Procedure:
   a. Boil the brown rice for 45 minutes and set aside. Heat the oil in a non-stick pan and add the finely chopped shallot. Brown and add the diced pumpkin. Cook for 5 minutes with the addition of 2 ladles of hot broth, then add the black cabbage cut into strips and cook for 10 minutes. Take the whole rice put aside and dip it in the pan with pumpkin and black cabbage for 5 minutes.

CHAPTER 6

SELF-PRODUCED VEG SLICED MEATS

1. Veg Salsiccia

Ingredients:
- 3½ oz of dried tomatoes
- 3 cloves of garlic
- paprika
- ¾ oz of linseed
- ¾ oz of pumpkin seeds
- 2 oz of sunflower seeds
- Halls

Procedure:
a. Soak the dried tomatoes. When they are soft, squeeze them out and put them in the mixer with the rest of the ingredients. Blend. Then, I think it's better to have a little grainy dough so don't reduce it to very fine dough. The consistency must be very very dense, do not try to add water! If it does not blend well, chop
b. with minipimmer. Then create the sausage, put it in baking paper and let it rest in the fridge overnight.
c. Next day you can cut it without any problems. I ate it with pickles prepared in summer, mustard and homemade bread today with flour from Iervicella and Solina. Ancient grains of Marche.

2. Sliced Soya Beans

Ingredients:
- 1 jar of natural soy beans

- Spicy garden hose 3 cm.
- 2 mancholes of curls of bran
- 2 level teaspoons of powdered agar agar (Rapunzel)
- 1 level teaspoon of locust bean gum
- 2/3 cup of vegetable broth
- 2 cups of cold water coffee
- salt, pepper to taste
- 1 teaspoon dried oregano
- 1 clove of garlic (optional)
- 2 teaspoons of ketchup

Procedure:

a. Pour into the blender's jar the soy beans, the curls of bran, the spicy Ortolina, the garlic, the oregano, the ketchup and the blends. Season with salt and pepper, then transfer 3 tablespoons of the very dense mixture you have obtained into a pot and add the broth little by little, creating a semi-liquid amalgam. Dissolve the agar agar and the carob bean gum in 2 cups of cold water and set aside the mixture. Put the pot over the heat and let the soybean cream boil, stirring occasionally with a wooden spoon: at this point, lower the heat of the stove to a minimum and pour into the pot the mixture of agar agar, water and locust bean gum. Stir continuously for 2 minutes - no more - after the boiling starts again, then remove the pot from the heat and pour the steaming cream into an oiled cylindrical mould. Wait 10 minutes (the time to cool down is not enough) and then put the mold in the fridge for 3-4 hours. After this time, the mixture will have solidified and you can slice it thinly to stuff your sandwiches!

3. Salamini Veg

Ingredients:

- 7 oz of sliced and cooked mushrooms
- 2 tablespoons triathed onion
- 1 clove of garlic, chopped
- 8½ oz cooked borlotti beans (equivalent to one can)
- 3 dried tomatoes (without oil, the dried ones and just, then 6 halves)
- 2½ oz of rice flour
- 1 tablespoon tamarisk
- 1 tablespoon apple vinegar
- black pepper
- paprika
- cinnamon

Procedure:

a. Put mushrooms, onion, garlic and borlotti in the blender and start to turn until the cream is a little irregular. In the meantime, chop the dried tomatoes without soaking them and add them to the blender, letting it go until the mixture becomes sufficiently creamy. Remove the mixture from the blender and move it to a bowl, add tamari, vinegar and spices according to personal taste. Mix well to mix well the flavors. Well, at this point the mixture is still too liquid so start to add the rice flour slowly stirring well, at the end it will still be wet but manageable. Prepare the steam cooker with a little water and with the mixture prepare some sausages with the help of the food film to make them more regular. Cook for 30 minutes in a steam cooker. Once cooked, be careful! Do not handle them, they are still too soft. Let the basket cool down with the salamis inside and when it can be handled place it in the fridge for the night. The next day they will be manageable, slicable and very good!

4. Yubacetta

Ingredients:

- 1¾ oz of dried yuba (213.75 kcal, 475/100 g kcal)
- smoked paprika qb
- paprikca forte qb

Procedure:

a. Soak the yuba with the aromas for at least 24 hours. Cook the yuba in a pan with the soaking water until the liquid is all dry. Cut the cooked yuba finely as in the photo.

5. Sliced With Seitan And Lentils

Ingredients:

- 4 oz instantaneous seitan
- 3½ oz lentil flour
- water qb
- a few pinches of salt
- 1/2 teaspoon ginger
- 1/2 teaspoon paprika
- 1 sprig of thyme
- 1 sprig of marjoram
- 2 sage leaves
- 1 sprig of rosemary
- 1 dry tomato

- 1 carrot
- 1 onion
- 2 tablespoons of soy sauce
- 1 piece of Kombu seaweed

Procedure:
   a. Pour 1 glass of water into a bowl, add the instant seitan, lentil flour, a pinch of salt, ginger, paprika, thyme, marjoram, rosemary, finely chopped sage, mix well with a fork then with your hands; if necessary add a little water to obtain a firm dough. Form a cylinder and roll into a white cloth closed at the end with kitchen string. Put on the heat a pot with 1.5 liters of water, add the carrot, onion, dried tomato, seaweed, soy sauce and, when it boils, add the salami; cover and cook for 35 minutes. Allow to cool in the broth, then cut thin with the slicer. Excellent as an appetizer.

6. Salamel

Ingredients:
- 8 oz of cannellini beans cooked in vegetable broth
- 18 oz of cooking water from the beans
- 14¾ oz gluten powder
- 3 teaspoons of fine pink salt
- 1 level teaspoon of black pepper
- 5 level teaspoons of brown sugar
- 2 level teaspoons of dried marjoram powder
- 2 level teaspoons of dried sage powder
- 2 level teaspoons of sweet paprika
- 2 level teaspoons of powdered onion
- 2 level teaspoons of garlic powder

Procedure:
   a. To prepare the salamella, put the cooked beans in the mixer and puree them, then add the gluten, spices and finally everything else. It will form a very elastic dough (even too much!) because of the presence of gluten. Meanwhile, prepare many squares of transparent film that you will need to cook the sausages and simultaneously gives them the classic sausage shape. Pour the mixture onto a pastry board, form an approximate roll with your hands and take one piece of the mixture at a time. You have to form a cylinder that you will place in the center of the square of film. Then roll it up as tight as you can and finally close the sides by twisting the film like a candy.

b. When they have cooled down, you can put them in the fridge without discarding them and store them like this, in an airtight container, at least 2-3 days. This operation is the most delicate and difficult because gluten is rather stubborn and overbearing: he wants to win! But fatigue is always rewarded with a truly impressive result. As you prepare them, put all the candies in the baskets of the steamer and cook for 30 minutes. When you serve them, all you have to do is cook them for a few more minutes on a hot grill or plate, taking care to turn them so that they form those pretty burnished strips, classic of grills.

7. Mopur

Ingredients:

- 4 oz of gluten flour
- 2 oz of chickpea flour
- 2 teaspoons of dried oregano
- 1 beautiful grated nutmeg
- 1 teaspoon of ground black pepper
- 2 tablespoons of food-grade yeast in flakes
- 2 tablespoons of soy sauce
- 1 tablespoon evo oil
- water qb
- vegetable broth

Procedure:

a. First make a nice tasty vegetable broth. While boiling, mix in a bowl gluten, chickpea flour, oregano, nutmeg, pepper, baking powder and add soy sauce, oil and water a little at a time, until you form a nice compact dough, not too soft. When the broth is ready, roll the dough into a gauze and close it on the sides with string. Cook in the broth for about 1 hour and 30 minutes over very low heat and with the lid. Finally unroll the mopur and leave it in the broth until it cools down. I then cut it into thin slices and put it in its cooking broth to flavor again!

8. Soyacetta

Ingredients:

- 1 oz of soya chuncks Trs (kcal 80.1, kcal 267/100 g)
- 3½ oz of shoyu (kcal 60, kcal 60/100 g)
- ½ cup of water
- 1 pinch of cayenne pepper
- 1 pinch of smoked paprika

Procedure:

a. Soak the chunks in water and shoyu in the microwave for 3 minutes at 950W. Cut the hydrated chunks as finely as possible so that they can absorb the remaining liquid as much as possible. Leave to soak for a few hours, covering with a weight to facilitate absorption. Squeeze the pieces of soya and spread them on a plate so that they do not overlap too much.

b. Add the spices by massaging the pieces of soya so that they absorb the spices well. Bake in the oven with a grill function for about 10 minutes and in any case until the desired degree of drying.

Considerations:

a. With these doses and with the degree of drying obtained were 65 g of soot with a calculation of calories (a little complicated, but I think correct) of 174/100 g kcal. Another version of soyacetta, a little spicier and saltier, is obtained using turmeric and pepper, tandoori masala, cayenne pepper and salt.

9. Tofucetta

Ingredients:

- 12 oz of frozen hard tofu (kcal 255, kcal 77/100 g)
- 2 oz of shoyu (kcal 39.6, kcal 60/100 g)
- 1/14 oz of smoked paprika
- 1/7 oz of tandoori masala
- 1/14 oz of garlic powder (kcal 1.8, kcal 90/100 g)
- pepper

Procedure:

a. Thaw the tofu: 8 oz of tofu will be thawed and wrung out. Keep the tofu water because that's where you have to mix the spices and shoyu, mixing well. Cut the tofu into small cubes and marinate for at least 1 hour in the prepared sauce. Bring everything to cooking on a stone plate (or non-stick pan) and let the liquid dry. Continue to toast until the desired crunchiness, adjusting, if necessary, salt or pepper.

Considerations:

a. Tot 4 oz cooked and cooled kcal 296 (i.e. kcal 249/100 g). It is not the best vegan bacon I have made. The taste is really spicy and smoky bacon, but tends to soften in cooking, and that's what has not satisfied me. So I would say that tofucetta is good for stuffing sandwiches or seasoning vegetables. You should try it on a pizza or a flan like Rusticotta ai denti de cagn.

10. Yoba Salami

Ingredients:

- 3 sheets of dry yuba (soaked in boiling water for 20 minutes)
- 2 tablespoons of soya cream
- 1 1/2 tablespoon of flakes of baking powder
- 1 teaspoon ginger powder
- 1 teaspoon of lemon juice
- salt, white pepper to taste
- 1 teaspoon of white wine
- 1 tablespoon of powdered agar agar (Rapunzel)
- 2/3 cup of water
- 1 teaspoon of wheat germ
- Ingredients for marinating:
- soy sauce to taste
- 2 tablespoons of Evo oil

Procedure:

Soak the sheets of yuba in oil and soy sauce for 15 minutes, then squeeze them and roll them up to form a sausage that you will wrap tightly in a piece of flax and steam for 20 minutes. Now dissolve the agar in the veg broth and pour the gel obtained in the jug of the blender, then blend the yuba with all the other ingredients and transfer the mixture over a low heat in a saucepan. Let it cook until it starts to boil, then wait 2 minutes and turn off the stove. Transfer the cured meat cream into an oiled container and, once it has cooled down, refrigerate to solidify, for 3-4 hours.

11. Yellow Salami

Ingredients:

- 5 oz boiled cannellini beans (also canned)
- 1 clove of red garlic
- 1½ oz of smoked tofu
- ¾ cup of salted vegetable broth
- 1 teaspoon of turmeric
- 1 tablespoon mustard in a tube
- chopped parsley at will
- 1 pinch of black pepper
- 2 cm of garlic paste in a tube
- 1 tablespoon of baking powder
- 1 pinch of cardamom
- 1 teaspoonful of agar agar
- 1 teaspoon of locust bean gum
- 1 tablespoon evo oil

- 1 cup of cold water

Procedure:

a. Crush the garlic clove and fry it in a small pot, in the olive oil, for 1 minute, then remove it and add the cannellini beans, letting them flavor for 1 minute. Remove the saucepan from the heat and add the yeast, smoked tofu, garlic paste, mustard and spices. Dissolve the locust bean gum in the broth, then pour it into the saucepan and mix everything with the minipimer, then put the pan back on the very low heat, stirring continuously the mixture that will thicken quickly. Dissolve the agar in cold water, mixing strongly with a teaspoon until you get a brown gel that you will pour into the pan. As soon as the concoction reaches the boil, wait 2 minutes always stirring, with the flame of the stove at minimum and then complete with oil and chopped parsley, before removing the pot from the heat and transfer the contents into an oiled mold, letting it cool before putting it in the refrigerator, for at least 2 hours, in order to allow it to solidify.

12. Barbos

Ingredients for the slipper:

- 1 jar of cooked chickpeas
- 1 handful of fresh or frozen fried vegetables
- 1 l of lukewarm, tasty vegetable broth
- beet juice
- 1 cup of smoked black tea Lapsang Souchong
- full-bodied red wine qb (non-acidic, vegan ok)
- salt
- white pepper qb (or black, make vobis)
- 1 teaspoonful of locust bean gum
- 1 teaspoonful of agar agar powder
- 1 sigh of garlic paste
- 2 tablespoons of oil evo (plus qb to grease the mold)
- 1 empty 500 ml yogurt container

Ingredients for the rooted meat:

- 1 jar of boiled borlotti beans
- 1 handful of vegetables per fried
- dried rosemary qb (optional)
- salt
- 1 generous dose of black pepper
- 1 pinch of garlic paste
- beet juice qb

- 1 teaspoonful of locust bean gum
- 1 teaspoonful of agar agar powder
- 2 tablespoons of oil evo (plus qb to grease the mold)
- 1 empty 500 ml yogurt container

Slut courtesy of the tramp:

a. After browning the vegetables for fried in oil in a suitable saucepan, pour the chickpeas drained from their preserving liquid, letting them season for 2 minutes, then water with red wine and let it evaporate. Season with salt and pepper and add 1 ladle of vegetable stock, letting the legumes cook over a low heat for about 10 minutes. When you see that the mixture "pulls", turn off the stove.

b. Add to the preparation the locust bean gum, garlic, beet juice (the amount that will drain from a pack of 500 g of boiled beets) and blend everything with the minipimer immersion, then put back on the heat (low) pot and its contents, add 4 tablespoons of black tea Lapsang Souchong and stir everything carefully and continuously. Melt the agar agar powder in 1 1/2 cup of coffee filled with cold water, then pour the gel obtained in the pot, mixing the chickpea cream and wait 2 minutes, always stirring, before removing the pan from the heat and pour the mixture into an oiled mold that you will transfer to the refrigerator, to solidify, for 3-4 hours.

Procedure for the Sloth:

a. Brown the vegetables in oil, in a suitable saucepan, for fried, then pour the beans drained from their liquid, minus 2 tablespoons that you will keep aside: they will be the eyes of the barbadella! Add 1 ladle of vegetable broth and let the beans go over a low heat for about 10 minutes. When you see that the mixture "pulls", turn off the stove. Add to the preparation the locust bean gum, the garlic paste, the beet juice (the quantity that will drain from a pack of 500 g of boiled beets) and mix everything with the immersion minipimer, then put back on very low heat the pot and its contents, stirring continuously. Add the previously drained whole beans and incorporate them into the mixture over the heat, stirring again; after which dissolve the agar agar in 1 1/2 cup of coffee filled with cold water and pour the gel obtained in the pot, mixing it with the cream of legumes. Cook for another 2 minutes, stirring constantly, before removing the pan from the heat and transfer the preparation in an oiled mould that will be placed in the fridge, to solidify, for 3-4 hours.

13. Wurstel

Ingredients:

- 5 1/3 oz of wheat gluten
- 1½ oz of broad bean flour
- 1½ oz of pea flour
- 4 tablespoons of baking powder
- 2 tablespoons of Evo oil
- spice cocktail to taste
- 1 teaspoon of turmeric
- 1 teaspoon of agar agar
- smoked salt qb
- vegetable broth qb

Request:

a. Combine all the flours and spices in a large bowl and mix; add oil and water to form a compact, but not hard, dough. Wrap in film for at least 2 hours, I 1 whole night, and keep in the refrigerator. Take out and form small cylinders that we will close with a candy in the foil, with this dose I have come 10. Take a pot with vegetable broth, or water and veg cube, and cold dip the packages; from the boil go like this for 1/2 hour. Pull the pot away from the heat and, with the help of a pliers and being careful not to burn, take the sausages, remove the foil and put them back into the broth, cook another 1/2 hour and let cool. I recommend that if you do not cook them immediately do not do like me that I put them in a dish without liquid: they tend to dry out! At this point they are ready to be grilled again and eaten as we did: purple cap finely chopped and cooked with apple vinegar and herb salt.

Considerations:

a. I divided this dough into small cylinders for the simple fact that so my baby takes them in hand without being there to "quarrel" with the fork, but no one takes away from cooking it in a single block. Next time we'll do them directly back into the peppers.

14. White Dinner

Ingredients:

- 1 ¼ cups of silken tofu
- 1 tablespoon full of soya yogurt
- salt, pepper to taste
- 1 teaspoonful of locust bean gum
- 2 teaspoons of agar agar powder

- 1 cup of cold water
- Seed oil for the mould

Ingredients for the cheese version:

- 3 scoops of soya milk powder plus 200 ml of water (or 200 ml of veg milk)
- 1 tablespoon of lemon juice
- 1 tablespoon vegetable cream
- 1 teaspoon full of flakes of baking powder

Ingredients for the cured meat version:

- ¾ cup of salted vegetable stock
- 1 tablespoon of vegan green olive pate
- 1 tablespoon of vegan mayonnaise
- 1 teaspoon full of sweet mustard

Procedure:

a. Pour the silken tofu and the locust bean gum into a saucepan, add the vegetable milk to produce the cold cheese or broth, if you opt for the cured meat, and heat the amalgam on the stove to a minimum, stirring continuously. Season with salt and pepper (in the sliced version you can add plenty!) and, just before the boiling point, add the optional ingredients, continuing to stir well. Dissolve the agar agar completely in 1 cup of coffee filled with cold water and add this mixture to the mixture over the heat. Let it cook for another 2 minutes, after which turn off the heat and pour the thick white cream into a container or mould greased with seed oil, before transferring it to the fridge for a few hours to compact. Cured meats or cheese? It's up to you to choose

15. Sliced With Lentils

Ingredients:

- 1 box of canned lentils (possibly organic)
- mixed for deep-frozen fried or celery, carrot and diced onion
- 1 tablespoon of light peppers
- About 1 ¼ cups of salted vegetable broth
- 1 tablespoon of tomato puree
- 1 teaspoon of agar agar
- 1 level teaspoon of locust bean gum
- 1 pinch of garlic paste
- the juice of 1/2 lemon
- salt, pepper to taste
- chilli to taste
- oil evo qb

Procedure:

a. Prepare the vegetable stock and keep it aside. Put the vegetables in a saucepan, with 2 tablespoons of oil, to brown. Add the previously drained canned lentils, the tomato puree, the salt to taste and leave to stew, serving, if necessary, with a little water. Blend the lentils with the minipimer and put them back in the pan. Dissolve the locust bean gum in the broth, using the minipimer, then add the minipimer to the lentil purée and put the saucepan on the stove. Stir carefully to avoid that the mixture, which will soon thicken, does not stick to the bottom of the pot. Boil the preparation for 5 minutes, then add the Peperonata light, or other to your taste, a generous amount of pepper, chilli, lemon juice and ... do not forget the usual pinch of garlic, however, is essential! Dissolve the agar agar in 1/2 cup of water and pour the mixture into the pot, stirring well. After 2 minutes from the resumption of boiling, turn off the stove and decant as usual the veg-salume in a plastic container greased with oil that you put in the refrigerator to solidify for 5-6 hours.

16. Salami Wonder

Ingredients:

- Granular broth qb
- 1 can of red beans
- gomasio qb
- pepper
- paprika qb
- curcuma qb
- 2 cloves of garlic
- 1 shallot
- 1 white onion
- 1 chilli (if desired)
- aromatic herbs at will
- breadcrumbs qb
- 2 tablespoons of soya lecithin soup
- 2 soup spoons of balsamic vinegar
- 2 tablespoons of soy sauce soup
- 1/2 glass of white wine
- water qb
- oil qb

Procedure:

a. Thinly slice 1 clove of garlic and shallot, pour a little oil into the pan and prepare the soffrittino with a little chopped herbs. Add the canned beans and sauté for a few minutes, adding a little soy sauce. In the meantime, mix a little granular broth with 1 glass of cold water. When the beans start to peel, add some water with the broth and cover until the beans almost "spatasciano". In a separate glass, pour the 2 tablespoons of lecithin and cover just with water (the water must slightly exceed the lecithin).

b. When the beans are nice to spatula, let them cool a little then pour them into a bowl where you will also add the breadcrumbs, finely sliced onion, other herbs, chopped paprika, turmeric, pepper and gomasio. Stir until you make a compact but soft "mash". Add at this point the lecithin that in the meantime has become sticky and continue to stir. Roll out a sheet of aluminium paper and on top of it a sheet of greased oven paper, soaked in water and squeezed. Pour in the mixture, roll it up and close it well. Boil for 45-60 minutes. I used a toothpick to find out if it was ready (it must be hard, but malleable). When cooked, cool and then open. In a large non-stick pan, pour the remaining oil, add the other chopped clove of garlic and brown. In the meantime, wrap the roll in the medical gauze and fasten with the food string.

c. In a glass mix wine, soy sauce and balsamic vinegar. Put the roll in a pan, brown well on all sides, wet with the remaining stock (which must be very little). When the broth is almost dry, raise the heat, sprinkle with the mixture of wine, soy sauce and balsamic vinegar, fade and cover for another 2 minutes. Et voilà, "se magna"!

Considerations:

a. I think this is the dish that has given me the most satisfaction, my boyfriend even before tasting it has looked at it and says to me "but are you crazy, are you doing the bagpipes? And what do you eat, sorry?"... Moroso carnivore deceived -mission accomplished! Obviously then I unveiled the "mystery"! At first I wanted to slice it like the sliced veg, then the taste reminded me a bit of that of the meat, the shape and color were those of the salami ... so here's the title! The taste was almost similar to that of the meat that my mother used to make every Christmas, even if the taste of the beans is quite full-bodied... Then it also depends very much on the spices and herbs used...

17. Wurstel Type 2

<u>Ingredients:</u>

- 1 tablespoon of barley flour (buckwheat for the gluten free version)
- 1 teaspoon of locust bean gum
- 1 teaspoon of agar agar
- 5 1/3 oz of boiled borlotti beans (also canned)
- vegetables for diced fried (also frozen)
- 250 ml of salted vegetable broth
- 1 teaspoonful of garlic paste
- 1 handful of stoned green olives
- 1 tablespoon of soy sauce (optional)
- 1 tablespoon of pickled peppers in listerelle cut into small pieces
- oil evo qb
- water qb
- salt, pepper to taste
- chilli to taste

Procedure:

a. Fry the diced vegetables in a little oil, then add the borlotti beans and season with salt, leaving them to simmer for a few minutes (add a small amount of water if necessary). Prepare the vegetable stock in the indicated quantity, so that it is quite tasty and let it cool down, after which dissolve the locust bean gum. With the help of a minipimer reduce the borlotti in puree directly in the saucepan and after adding the barley flour and broth, put it on the stove and boil it for 10 minutes. Dissolve the agar agar in a little water and add the mixture to the contents of the saucepan stirring continuously. Now is the time to add the sliced olives, the chopped pepper fillets and all the remaining flavours. After 2 minutes, with minimum heat, turn off the heat and pour the cream obtained in a previously oiled mold, before putting in the refrigerator, to solidify, for a few hours (I waited all 1 night).

18. Trasure Dinner

Ingredients:

- 9 1/3 oz of natural tofu
- 1¾ oz of instant seitan
- 3 cups of tomato puree
- 2 cups of pistachios
- 1 cup of sesame
- 1 cup of fennel seeds
- 1 cup of alimentary yeast
- 1 cup of sunflower oil

- 1 oz of dried tomatoes
- 4 oz of soy milk
- 2 cups of agar agar powder
- 1 cup ginger powder
- 1 cup of shoyu
- 1 cup of chilli oil evo
- Ingredients for the sauce:
- 6 cups of white soya yoghurt
- 1 cup of tahin
- 1/2 cup mustard
- 1 cup of chilli oil evo
- 1 cup of balsamic vinegar
- 1 cup of shoyu
- 1 cup ginger powder
- 1 cup of rice miso
- soy milk qb

Procedure:

a. First reduce the pistachios and sesame powder to a powder, then transfer them together with all the other ingredients except the instant seitan into the blender. Operate the blades for several minutes making the necessary intervals not to stress it and then when everything is perfectly blended add the instant seitan blending only the time necessary to mix it with the rest, but no more for its tendency to make the compound immediately very "often". Transfer the result to a white cloth sterilized with boiling water and never washed with detergent, give it the shape of a salamot, tie it at the ends and also for its length with kitchen string and boil it for about 1 hour in a broth prepared with carrots, onions, celery and 2 tablespoons of shoyu. Let it cool in the broth and only when it is well cold unwind it from the cloth and cut it into slices. Here it is in all its glory.

b. It can be stored for 3-4 days in the fridge in the cooking broth in a frigoverre, but it is also excellent frozen. Give me another shot as it is the first sliced self-produced.

19. Salami Red

Ingredients:
- 2 oz of instant seitan
- 1 piece of tofu for fat pellets
- 1¾ oz of chickpea flour
- oil qb
- 1 red pepper

- 3 dried tomatoes in oil
- 1 pot of broth
- salt
- chilli to taste

Procedure:

   a. First of all steam the red pepper, once cooked blend it, also blend the dried tomatoes and put everything in a bowl together with the rest of the ingredients. Knead with your hands and give the shape of a salami, wrap it in a dish towel and put to cook in the broth for 30 minutes; once cooked, remove from the dish towel and leave to cool and then sprinkle with flour to give the idea of the salami. Put in the fridge. I had it for lunch at work with bread and veg mayonnaise.

   b. Very good! The idea of the non-vegan is that it had the taste of the Calabrian anduja.

20. Smoked Salami

Ingredients:
- 1 bag of instant seitan
- about 3½ oz of smoked tofu (a little less than 1/2 loaf)
- ariosto (or any flavoured salt)
- water
- vegetable broth

Procedure:

   a. Blend the smoked tofu with water until it becomes very creamy. In a bowl put the instant seitan, add the blended tofu, the ariosto (I like it very much, I use it almost everywhere, but also a mixture of herbs or spices to which add salt) and water just enough to mix everything (I used a little more than 1/2 glass). If you used ariosto you don't need salt, if you use a mix of herbs or spices add salt. Knead well, wrap the dough in a cotton cloth and form the salami (tying the edges with kitchen string as if it were a candy).

   b. Cook in a large pot with some vegetable broth (I prepared it with a carrot, a shallot, two bay leaves, a stalk of celery, a piece of ginger and a little salt) for at least half an hour from when the boil starts (I put it cold).

   c. Turn off the gas, let it cool down just enough not to burn you. Remove it from the cloth and put it to dry on a grid (a chopping board is also fine, just turn it every now and then so that the part in contact does not remain wet). Let cool completely and cut into slices.

21. Homemade Salami

Ingredients:

- 2 oz of instant seitan
- 1 piece of tofu (to make "fat" pellets)
- 1 pinch of peppercorns
- 1¾ oz of chickpea flour
- 2 tablespoons of oil
- halls
- 1 tablespoon of tomato paste
- water qb
- 1 pot of broth

Procedure:

a. In a bowl, mix the seitan with the salt, the chickpea flour, the chopped tofu and the peppercorns. Add the tomato paste, oil and water (usually half a glass is enough, but it depends on the brand of gluten you use). Mix well with your hands, so as to spread evenly the red color of the sauce. Close in a dish towel giving it the shape of a sausage and boil for at least half an hour in plenty of vegetable broth (I have also added some soy sauce). When the cooking is over, rinse it under cold water, strip it of the dishcloth and let it dry.

22. Trust Dinner

Ingredients:

- eggplant
- sweet potato
- round courgettes
- yellow zucchini
- red onions
- carrots, leek
- peppers
- potatoes
- mushrooms
- red turnips
- tomatoes
- saucepans
- spinach
- basil
- mint

- breadcrumbs
- good oil

Procedure:

a. Clean all the vegetables.

b. Cook over high heat, without fat and add the oil when cooking is almost complete, the leafy vegetables (spinach) and basil and mint add them at the last minute, organize yourself with large pots. When the vegetables are cooked and the greased kitchen cut everything with a knife until it is pureed (on the tip of a knife!!!), adding breadcrumbs to give compactness; in fact Francesco started from the technique used by those who make the cruel sausages and, to invite us to lunch with him, he used the same technique to make a gift: and what a gift! Give the shape to the dough with the help of the food film, spread a nice strip of film on the worktop, start to place the dough on the long side about 10 cm from the edge, then start to roll up the film starting on one side and advancing until you finish on the other. Care must be taken to roll up the dough, but not to let the film enter the dough: when the film is unrolled, it will form anti-aesthetic folds. Decide the length you want to give to the "sausage" of vegetables finished and at that point tighten the roll with your fingers to make room and roll up the 2 pieces in the opposite direction to each other, to do this more easily and avoid that the dough comes out you have to leave a little empty film at the beginning and end of the roll.

23. Salami With Puttanesca Cheese

Ingredients:

- Twice as much as those used by Conci in sliced vegetable with some modification.
- 5 1/3 oz of organic tofu
- 1 tablespoon of powdered oatmeal or organic oatmeal
- 6 or 7 level spoons of instant seitan or fresh seitan blended bio
- 3 teaspoons of potato starch (I didn't have cornstarch)
- 2 teaspoons of organic agar agar
- 2 tablespoons of organic flakes of food-grade yeast
- 3 tablespoons of Evo oil
- 1 tablespoon of organic tomato puree
- 1 teaspoon of soy sauce
- for flavoring: A pinch of strong paprika and chili pepper, Mediterranean oregano, curry, garlic
- (abundant), onion flakes and olives stoned into small pieces.

Procedure:

a. Predict the tofu, and instead of blending it, reduce it to cream with a fork (there will be some whole white pieces that remind you of the salami, as you can see in the picture) along with oil, soy sauce, yeast and spices to flavor.

b. Add the tomato puree and then all the dried ingredients sieved and finally the olives in small pieces, mixed well first with the fork, then with your hands. Now give it the shape of a salami.

c. Now, as usual, prepare a broth with sage, and from the moment of boiling let your sage steam for 30/40 minutes.

d. Once cooked, let it cool... Once warm or cold, slice it into thin slices, place the slices on a plate and put a few hours in the fridge. (I prepared it last night, to make my Adry taste it today!)

e. As he liked it, today at lunch he ate a risotto with diced salami, olives and chopped tomatoes... A drizzle of oil evo.

24. Fairy Salami

Ingredients:

- 2 oz of broad bean flour
- 1¾ oz of gluten (instant seitan)
- 2 tablespoons of potato starch
- ginger powder
- dry dill
- dry rosemary
- chili
- nutmeg
- fenugreek
- cilantro
- onion (preferably powdered)
- evo qb
- 1/4 cup of hot water
- 1 teaspoon of Trocomare

Procedure:

a. Small premise for those who do not have broad bean flour. I did this: I pulverized the dried broad beans that had been peeled and broken up in the chopper. All you need is patience. To flavor the gluten I took the spices, all used in small quantities - more ginger and dill - and I put them in the shredder along with 3 tablespoons of gluten. The rest of the instant seitan I mixed with the aromatic salt. Then I combined the spicy gluten with the salty one, the broad bean flour, the starch and I mixed everything with a spoon.

b. I added the onion (I had not dried it so I first chopped it and then reduced it to puree in the blender), a little 'oil and 60 ml of hot water (important factor!) from the tap. I stirred everything vigorously by hand (following the same verse) with a whisk with the ends in love, until the gluten has absorbed all the water and has thickened well. I formed a ball and let it rest for about twenty minutes. I then took it and worked it lightly with my hands and stuffed it in the transparent film, tightening the ends with the film itself and with kitchen string. In a nutshell: a candy clasp. I put the salamot in the fridge for a day. Here it is freed from the film. As you can see, it is already very compact. Placing between the salamot and the basket a porcelain plate resistant to high temperatures (a plate of ceramic or pyrex is also fine). The dish is served to prevent it from sticking to the basket. Above the basket to cook better, I put a glass lid.

c. After 40 minutes, I let it cool and dry at room temperature and again wrapped in clear film and refrigerated for a day.

d. Now the salami is ready to be sliced on a cutting board with a nice serrated bread knife.

25. Sliced Happy

Ingredients for a small "roll" of sliced vegan:

- 2¾ oz of fresh tofu (I've always used the homemade one, I don't know if with the one I bought I can do it anyway, the texture and the taste are different)
- 2 teaspoons of oat flakes reduced to a powder with a grinder or coffee grinder and sieved (5 gr.)
- 3 level tablespoons of instant seitan (25 gr.)
- 1 teaspoon of cornstarch (3 gr.)
- 1 and a half tablespoons of manitoba flour (15 gr.)
- 1/2 teaspoon agar agar
- 1 tablespoon of yeast in flakes (4 gr.)
- 1/2 tablespoon miso rice (3 gr.)
- 1 and a half tablespoons of sunflower oil
- 1 teaspoon of tamarisk
- 1 small piece of crumbled stock cube (3 gr.)

For flavouring:

- Small amounts of freshly chopped
- parsley, basil, mint

- grated lemon peel
- tiny pieces of dried tomatoes and carrot
- a pinch of: ginger, nutmeg, coriander powder, onion flakes, pepper.

Procedure:

a. Blend the tofu with oil, miso, tamari and cube until it is creamy, add all the flavourings ("to flavour") and blend again. Add all the dry ingredients and blend or knead with your hands. After mixing everything well, form a roll with your hands, grease it with a little oil and wrap it tightly in a wet cloth, as you do for seitan. Close by knotting the two ends with string and put it to cook in boiling water for about 35 min.

b. After this time, remove the cloth and let it cool down. Do not slice it immediately, it must first cool and harden.

c. When it is cold, slice it with a smooth blade knife and put it in the fridge. taste it after hours.

CHAPTER 7

VEGAN CHEESE

1. Stracchino Veg

Ingredients:
- 9 oz of wholemeal cooked rice
- 3½ oz of soya yoghurt
- 1/2 cup soy milk
- 2 teaspoons of Agar Agar
- 2 tablespoons of baking powder
- Juice of 1/2 lemon

Preparation:
a. Blend the cooked rice with the soy milk and the baking powder until a smooth and creamy mixture is obtained.
b. Transfer everything to a saucepan, heat to a sweet flame continuing to turn with a wooden spoon, then add the Agar Agar and cook until it boils, lastly add the lemon juice and soybean yogurt.
c. Let it thicken while maintaining a soft and creamy texture.
d. Switch off and transfer the mixture into glass or ceramic containers.
e. If you wish, before transferring the rice mixture into the container, you can also add freshly chopped herbs or spices according to your taste.
f. Let it rest in the refrigerator for 24 hours.
g. You can spread the Strachicco on toast, bread, baked potatoes and raw or cooked vegetables.
h. It can be stored in the refrigerator for 5 days.

2. Coccola

Ingredients:
- 3/4 cup of coconut milk
- 1 tablespoon full of cornstarch

- 1 tablespoon semolina
- 1 tablespoon peanut oil
- 1 teaspoon of coconut oil
- 2 teaspoons of agar agar powder (I, the one from Rapunzel)
- 2 1/2 glasses of water
- salt
- lemon juice bio qb

Procedure:

a. Disperse the cornstarch in 2 glasses of cold water and pour the mixture into a saucepan, then put it on low heat. When the heat approaches, add salt, semolina and coconut milk. Stir for about 10 minutes with minimum heat. Dissolve the agar agar in the remaining 1/2 glass of water and pour the gel obtained in the saucepan. Add the lemon juice and coconut oil. Stir continuously until the mixture, similar to a soft polenta, will not detach itself from the sides of the pan. At this point, it must be transferred into a mould previously oiled with seed oil (it will be fine a plastic tray or a cup) and put the container in the refrigerator, after about ten minutes, to solidify, for 4 hours. The vegan mozzarella obtained is good on its own and also on the pizza. In this case, just grate it on the surface of the pizza and bake it, activating the grill function of the oven, to see it melt.

3. Tris

Ingredients

- Base
- 3½ oz cashews
- 3½ oz almonds
- 1/2 teaspoon garlic powder
- 1 teaspoon miso
- 1 teaspoon salt
- 1 lemon (juice)
- 2/3 cup water
- 1 teaspoon apple vinegar (optional)
- 2 tablespoons of yeast in flakes
- 1/2 tablespoon tapioca flour (optional)

Seasonings:

- 5 leaves fresh basil
- 1 teaspoon turmeric powder
- 1 teaspoon smoked paprika
- 1 carrot (blanched)
- 2 tablespoons of water
- 10 dried tomatoes (not in oil)
- 1 tablespoon evo oil
- 1/4 cup of water

Procedure:

a. The evening before the preparation soak the cashews and almonds.

b. Start the preparation of the base by rinsing the oily fruit and placing it in the glass of a powerful blender or a food processor.
c. Add all the ingredients indicated for the base and, pouring the water a little at a time, blend until you get a smooth and creamy mixture. The consistency must be similar to that of a spreadable butter, not liquid but not even grainy. If necessary, add more water to obtain the desired consistency.

4. Raw Cheese

Ingredients:
- 5 1/3 oz of Cashew nuts (left in water for one night)
- 2 tablespoons of Evo Oil
- 1/3 oz of chopped thyme
- half a teaspoon of lemon juice
- pinch of pepper
- salt to taste
- handful of capers (without salt)

Procedure:
a. Blend all the ingredients in a blender.
b. Put the cheese obtained to pour into a formina by ricotta, I have 3 that I guard jealously, in the refrigerator for one night.
c. Cashew cheese is excellent to eat on croutons as an aperitif, to dress the pasta or to eat sliced, cooking, some capers and pepper.

5. Tofu

Ingredients for a 10 oz Tofu loaf:
- 6 oz organic yellow soybean
- 1 1/5 liters of water + 3½ oz soaking water
- 1/4 oz of nigari (magnesium chloride)

Required equipment (available directly from Amazon):
- Large pot with high edges
- Skimmer
- Powerful blender, I use the Bimby
- Bag for filtering vegetable milk
- Spindles
- Food scale
- Cloth
- It's important to have a powerful blender to get the best possible yield and not throw away precious nutrients.

Procedure:
a. Soak the soya for 1 night or at least 8 hours, but also 12 hours, changing the water at least a couple of times. Rinse the soy beans in the blender and blend at full speed for about 2 minutes, in half the

water. At this point filter the milk obtained using the bag and squeeze well, store in the fridge the okara (the dry residue filtered that you can use for other recipes).

b. Pour the liquid obtained in the pot and add the other 600 ml of water, in the meantime dissolve the nigari in 100 ml of water and keep aside. Now heat the milk, when it starts to boil and to increase in volume pour the water into the pot with the nigari and remove from the heat.

c. Stir slightly, cover the pot with the cloth and leave to rest for 15/20 minutes, at which point the milk will be completely curdled. With the help of the skimmer, transfer the curd into the twigs and let the whey drain. Now the tofu is ready, store it in a jar with a solution of water and salt (8 grams of salt for 1 litre of water), boil the tofu for a few minutes before consuming it.

6. Pumpkin Seed Cheese

Ingredients:

- 4 tablespoons of peeled pumpkin seeds
- 1 level teaspoon of creamy cren without adding cream
- 1 tuft of chopped chives
- 1 glass of water
- 1 cup of water for coffee (to dissolve the agar agar)
- 1 1/2 teaspoons agar agar powder (Rapunzel)
- salt
- 1 teaspoon peanut oil

Procedure:

a. Soak the pumpkin seeds in water for 4 hours and let them soften, then drain them, rinse them and put them in the blender's glass. Dissolve the agar agar powder carefully in a coffee cup of cold water, so that no lumps are formed and keep the mixture aside. Now let's go back to the pumpkin seeds in the blender and add the cren, oil, salt and a glass of water, little by little, until we get a fluid cream. Transfer the mixture into a small pan, which we will put on a low heat and start to stir. When the cream begins to thicken and simmer, lower the heat to a minimum and add the mixture of agar agar dissolved in the water we had kept aside and the chopped chives. Now stir continuously, while the mixture boils, for another 3 minutes, then move the pot away from the heat. Transfer the cheese mixture into a mould previously greased with oil and let it cool for 15 minutes, before putting it in the fridge to solidify, for at least 4 hours.

7. Veg Recipe

Ingredients:

- 4 cups of soy milk without sugar or additives (io Provamel)
- 1 cup of coffee with lemon juice
- 1 generous teaspoon of wholemeal salt

Procedure:
a. Put the soy milk in a saucepan and wait for the boiling, in the meantime prepare the lemon juice filtering it with a strainer.
b. As soon as the milk starts to boil, turn off the pot and immediately pour in the lemon juice and salt, stir quickly, cover with a lid and let it rest for at least 30 minutes, I usually forget it there for a few hours.
c. Then pour the mixture into a special ricotta cheese sprig and leave to rest in the fridge for 24 - 48 hours so that the ricotta loses all its liquid part.

8. Vegcheese

Ingredients:
- 5 1/3 oz of sunflower seeds soaked for a few hours,
- 2½ cups of water,
- 1 tablespoon of Evo oil (optional),
- 2½ oz of rice or maize starch,
- White pepper and garlic powder to taste.

Procedure:
a. Blend all the ingredients together, put on low heat for about 7 minutes and continue to stir. When it thickens pour into a bowl soaked in cold water and place in the refrigerator for about 3 hours.

Remarks:
a. It is suitable as a spreadable cheese on bread, pizza, trousers, has a delicate flavor, is not heavy, you can vary the composition by adding in place of a part of sunflower seeds: cashew nuts, peanuts, almonds, walnuts brasiliane, parsley and other flavors at will (parsley, turmeric, etc.) to have a vegan cheese with different flavors. It can be stored for more than a week in the refrigerator without any problems, unlike soya cheeses, which deteriorate more quickly if made at home. Instead of starch you can use chickpea flour or potato starch to get a softer version, varying the amount of thickener you can also get a softer cream to use as cream for lasagna or pasta, you can leave the imagination to get amazing results!

9. Almond Spreadable Cheese

Ingredients:
- waste from the production of almond milk or other oilseeds
- seed oil with a neutral flavour (maize germ, steam-deoded sunflower, grape seed)
- water
- pinch of salt

Tools:
- glass blender

Procedure:

a. Put the almond pulp in the jug, add two or three tablespoons of oil and two tablespoons of water, a pinch of salt and blend; when the blades lose contact with the mixture add oil or water of your choice to facilitate the flow of blending; continue to blend until the blades work continuously making the classic vortex (I found that it is called turbulence!!) and the mixture will begin to "assemble" slightly. Done!

10. Soya Ricotta

Ingredients for vegetable cheese:

- 2 cups of unsweetened soy milk
- lemon juice

Ingredients for the seasoning:

- Pink Himalayan salt
- linseed
- a few rocket leaves
- Preparation tools:
- tofu mould or cheese twig
- cotton gauze/towel (preferably white)

Procedure:

a. Put the soy milk in a saucepan on the fire, when it starts to boil turn off the flame and pour a tablespoon of lemon juice, the doses of lemon are indicative you adjust the amount when you begin to see that the milk creates the curd, that is, begins to shrink ... it is more difficult to say that to do actually. I was able to do it immediately from the first time, believe me it's really simple.

b. At this point let it rest for about an hour at room temperature to allow the curd to finish. Once the time is over, get a cotton or hemp gauze or any other fabric as long as it is made of natural fibres and not coloured unless you want a rainbow-coloured cheese and with a ladle and a strainer make the curd drip over the gauze. Some time ago I bought the tofu mould already provided with holes on the base, but a strainer and a plastic mould are also fine.

c. The final consistency of the cheese will be proportional to the time of dripping and how much pressure you make with the back of the spoon to ensure that the liquid comes out completely. The more it drips, the more you press, the more compact the consistency.

d. At this point you can put your vegetable cheese in the refrigerator and when you taste it season it as you like. I recommend the dressing because it has a fairly neutral taste (like the tofu of the rest), I have tasted it with salt oil linseed rocket and some tomatoes.

11. Moncaprice

Ingredients:

- 2 cubes of fresh brewer's yeast

- 2/3 cup of water (plus a cup to dissolve the agar agar)
- 2 tablespoons full of cornstarch
- ½ cup of unsweetened soya milk
- 1 teaspoon of margarine without palm oil
- 1 teaspoon of tahin
- 2 teaspoons full of agar agar powder (Rapunzel)
- 1/2 teaspoon of fine salt
- Seed oil (for greasing the mould)

Procedure:

a. Stemp the corn starch in 160 ml of water, mixing until you get a milky liquid that we will pour into a saucepan. Add the crushed brewer's yeast and let it melt well with the help of a spoon, then add the salt. Let's heat the soy milk up to the boiling point, then, using a plunger-shaped milk frother, transform it into a firm cream and keep it aside. Dissolve the agar agar completely in 1 cup of cold water and keep the resulting mixture on hand. At this point, put the saucepan on the stove, over a low heat, stirring continuously. As soon as the mixture begins to thicken, add the tahin and margarine and mix faster, then add the soy milk and adjust the flame to the minimum, allowing it to incorporate well into the mixture. Finally, when the cream cheese starts to boil, pour the agar agar previously melted into the saucepan and mix quickly for 2 minutes, then remove the pan from the stove and pour the mixture, which will appear fluid and homogeneous, in an oiled mold. After 15 minutes, transfer the mould to the fridge and let the veg-caciotta solidify properly for a whole night.

12. Tofulino

Ingredients:

- 1 x 180 g (6½ oz) solid tofu loaf
- 2 fresh sage leaves
- 2 teaspoons of garlic oil Evo
- 1 teaspoon of white vinegar
- 1 teaspoonful of agar agar powder (Rapunzel)
- salt
- 1 cup of coffee filled with cold water

Procedure:

a. Nothing could be simpler! Let's put everything in the blender and let's get it going for a few minutes, until we get a nice creamy mixture, which we will pour into a saucepan. Let's light the stove to a minimum and, by stirring, let's wait for the mixture to reach boiling point. At this point, always stirring, we cook it for 2 more minutes - no more - before turning off the stove and transfer the mixture into an oiled mold before that, after 1/4 of an hour, we can put in the refrigerator for 2 hours, so that the caciottina solidifies properly.

13. Canestrato Veg

Ingredients:

- 5 1/3 oz of vacuum-packed lupins
- 1 cube of fresh brewer's yeast
- 2 tablespoons of flakes of alimentary yeast
- 1 tablespoon of licoli sourdough (or soya white yoghurt)
- 1 tablespoon of rice oil
- 1 tablespoon of powdered agar agar (Rapunzel)
- 1 cup of water

Procedure:

a. Peel and rinse the lupins in fresh water, then reduce them to a fine cream with a blender, using 2-3 tablespoons of water (30 ml). Dissolve the agar agar carefully in 100 ml of cold water and keep the mixture aside. Dissolve the cube of brewer's yeast in the remaining 100 ml of water at room temperature and pour the mixture on the bottom of a saucepan. Then add the cream of lupins, the yeast in flakes, the spoonful of licoli sourdough, stir and cook over low heat. There is no need to add salt. After 2 minutes, add the mixture of agar and water, stir again and wait for the cream cheese to boil. At this point, pour in the rice oil and remove the pan from the heat. Now place a plastic cheese sprig (small size, for ricotta) in a cup that can contain it and pour in the veg cheese cream, as I show you in the picture below. Don't worry, only a few drops will come out from the holes of the spindle, while the mass will be retained.

14. Veggrana

Ingredients:

- 10 oz fresh brewer's yeast (152.32 kcal, 56/100 kcal)
- 1 1/3 oz gomashio (kcal 202.088, kcal 505.22/100 g)
- 2 oz of baking powder (kcal 207, kcal 345/100 g)
- 1/3 oz of dry dulse (kcal 14, kcal 140/100 g)
- 3/7 oz of salt
- 2½ oz of water
- 5/7 oz of agar agar (kcal 3.2 kcal 16/100 g)
- 1½ cups of water
- 1½ oz of white miso (kcal 85.5, kcal 190/100 g)

Ingredients for gomashi0:

- 3½ oz sesame (kcal 573, P 17.1 g, kcal 573/100 g, P17.1g/100 g)
- 1/3 oz of salt
- 1/7 oz of flaked nori (kcal 8, P 2.9, kcal 200/100 g, P 41,4 g/100 g)

Procedure:

a. Crumble the fresh yeast and add it to the baking powder, gomashio and dulse seaweed. Soften with 2½ oz of slightly warm water. Leave to rise/ferment in the oven off, but preheated to 40-50 ° for several hours, even all night, it's okay. When the volume of the mixture has almost tripled, dissolve the agar agar in 12½ oz of water and bring to a boil. Pour the still hot and liquid gelatine into the leavened mixture and mix very well and quickly before the gelatine becomes solid! Line a shape (I am the Frigoverre container) with transparent film: it must adhere well to the walls. Spread the miso evenly on the film. If the miso is too hard, soften it with a few drops of water or, better, of shoyu, which strengthens the umami flavor. Then pour the mixture and cover well with the edges of the film. Let cool and firm completely. Once cold, pour the cheese onto a plate and remove the film. Leave to air-dry until the miso has made a crust. I put it in the fridge (ventilated, like a cellar, but much colder than).

Considerations:
a. Tot 826 g cold and solid kcal 664.11, kcal 80.40/100 g. It is good immediately, but I strongly recommend eating it after at least 6 days of "seasoning". It has a solid, slightly spongy consistency. It is not flaked, but is broken with the fingers, grated, sliced with a knife and even with the electric slicer without "creaminess".

15. Mozzarella's Veg

Ingredients:
- 1 l of natural soy milk
- 3 tablespoons of yeast for food use
- 2/3 oz of potato starch
- 1/3 oz locust bean gum (otherwise add 10 g potato starch)
- 1/3 oz of sunflower oil
- 1 tablespoon coconut oil
- 1/6 oz of agar agar
- 1/9 oz onion powder
- 1/7 oz of salt

Procedure:
a. In a pot, add all the ingredients without forming lumps, pour in the liquids first and dissolve all the powders individually with a hand whisk. Once we have obtained the smooth and fluid mixture, bring to a boil and let it boil for 4-5 minutes over low heat, continuing to turn. Line the cups with transparent film and pour the liquid obtained, close them and keep them suspended, they must solidify at room temperature and take shape. Then transfer to the refrigerator at rest for 2-3 hours.

16. Coccocaciotta

Ingredients:
- 1¾ oz of coconut milk (1 jar like that of peeled tomatoes)
- 1 tablespoon tapioca starch
- 2 teaspoons of coconut oil
- 1 tablespoon liego (dry food yeast with gomasio)
- 1 teaspoon of tahin
- 4 tablespoons of crushed mechanical walnuts

- 1 tablespoon of powdered agar agar (Rapunzel)
- 1 cup of cold water
- salt, pepper to taste
- Seed oil (for greasing the mould)

Procedure:
a. Thoroughly dissolve the tapioca starch in the coconut milk and the agar agar in the cold water, then pour both mixtures into a saucepan, which you will put on a low heat. Stir continuously the mixture until you see it thicken: at this point lower the heat of the stove to a minimum and adjust salt and pepper. As soon as the cream cheese has started to boil, add the liego, tahin, coconut oil and, finally, the crushed walnuts. Stir for another minute quickly, to assemble the ingredients well together and allow the flavors to melt, then remove the pan from the heat. Transfer the cheese into an oiled mould and let it cool down, then refrigerate the container for a whole night, so that the vegan-cheese solidifies. Here is the walnut coccocaciotta just sformata ...

17. Mandorella

Ingredients:

- 3 oz of peeled almonds
- 2/3 cup of Naturattiva soy milk
- 2/3 cup of soya cream
- 2 oz of cornstarch
- 1 tablespoon of baking powder
- evo oil
- salt
- fresh chives
- sweet paprika
- pink pepper
- walnuts

Procedure:
a. Blend the almonds finely. Combine the chopped almonds, cornstarch, milk, cream, baking powder and salt in a saucepan. Mix well and cook over low heat until the mixture begins to detach from the sides of the pot. Grease 3 containers with olive oil and place walnuts, paprika, pepper and chives on the bottom. Divide the mixture into 3 parts. In one add the walnuts, in another chives and in the last ground pepper and paprika. Leave to rest in the fridge for about 6 hours.

18. Pumpkin Tofuricotta

Ingredients:

- 1 l of soy milk (better if self-produced)
- 1/2 lemon
- 2 slices of pumpkin
- 2 tablespoons of sunflower oil

- 1 teaspoon ginger powder
- halls
- 1 pinch of parsley

Procedure:

a. Steam the pumpkin. In a pot heat the soy milk (keep 1 glass aside), when it begins to smoke and to make the bubbles on the edges add the lemon juice. Turn off and let cool. In a blender, or with the minipimer, blend the pumpkin (with or without peel ... do it yourself), the glass of milk, oil, ginger, salt and parsley, until you get a cream. Pour the curdled milk into a finely woven strainer, or through a cotton cloth, to separate the tofu from the water. Drain well and then mix in a bowl with the pumpkin cream. Pour into 1-2 containers to drain the ricotta and put a weight that puts pressure (I put a glass full of water). Leave it in the fridge to drain, and know that the more you leave it there, the more compact it is.

19. Vegalpino

Ingredients:

- 1 cube of fresh brewer's yeast
- 4 teaspoons of soya lecithin
- 2 tablespoons of almond milk powder
- 4 teaspoons of sweet soya drink powder
- 1 tablespoon satin cornstarch
- 4 tablespoons of natural soya yoghurt
- 3/7 oz of cocoa butter (4 single-serve squares)
- 2 cups of water coffee
- salt

Procedure:

a. Collect the powdered almond milk, cornstarch and soya drink on the bottom of a saucepan and add the cold water in which you have dissolved the soya lecithin. Mix well, avoiding the formation of lumps, then add the crushed yeast and cocoa butter. Place the pan on very low heat (better still in a bain-marie) and you will see the ingredients melt, mixing together in a soft cream. Season with salt, mix and turn off the heat before adding the yoghurt. Mix it all gracefully and your cheese is good and ready!

20. Flower Malga

Ingredients:

- 2 level tablespoons of almond milk powder
- 3/4 cup of water
- 1 tablespoon of powdered agar agar (Rapunzel)
- 1/2 pack of soya cream
- 1 tablespoon of lemon juice
- 1 cube of brewer's yeast
- salt

- white pepper to taste
- 2 tablespoons of sunflower seeds
- 1 sprig of fresh rosemary
- 1 teaspoon of poppy seeds
- 1 pinch of psyllium seeds
- 1 teaspoon of pistachio flour
- 1 bay leaf

Procedure:

a. Collect the almond milk powder and agar agar in a saucepan and dissolve them carefully with a whisk in cold water. Put the pan over a low heat and add the brewer's yeast, soya cream, salt, pepper and lemon while stirring. Continue stirring until the mixture becomes creamy and slightly frothy. Before removing the saucepan from the heat, add half of the sunflower seeds and set aside the other half for the final decoration.

21. Cashew Mozzarella

Ingredients for cashew milk:

- 2 oz of unroasted and unsalted cashew nuts
- 3/4 cup and 2 tablespoons of water

Ingredients for mozzarella:

- cashew milk
- 2 tablespoons full of cornstarch
- 4 tablespoons full of water
- 1 teaspoon of soya butter coffee
- 1 teaspoon of soya cream coffee
- 1 tablespoon of lemon juice
- salt
- Seed oil (for greasing the mould)

Procedure for cashew milk:

a. I left the cashews to soak in water for one night, after which I blended everything finely with the minipimer in a plastic jug and added, at the end, a pinch of salt.

Procedure for the mozzarella:

a. I put the corn starch in a saucepan and dissolved it with cold water, then I added the amount of cashew milk I had obtained (suppergiú 1 glass of water full, taking into account that I had drunk a cup of coffee for tasting) and I put the pan on low heat, stirring continuously. As soon as the mixture began to thicken, I combined the soya butter, soya cream, a pinch of salt and finally the lemon juice. When the cheese mass started to come off the sides of the pan, I turned off the stove. I then decanted it into a cup greased previously with seed oil, leveling the surface with the back of a spoon soaked in cold water and let it cool before transferring it to the refrigerator to solidify for 4-5 hours.

22. Philadelpi Veg

Ingredients:

- 2/3 cup of soya yoghurt
- ½ cup of soy milk
- ½ cup of water
- 1 teaspoonful of potato starch flour
- 2 tablespoons of soya cream
- 1 tablespoon of agaranta
- 2 tablespoons of lemon juice
- salt
- Evo oil for greasing the mold
- Ingredients for flavoring:
- fresh chives
- walnuts
- squeezed garlic
- chili
- sweet paprika
- green apple

Procedure:

a. Dissolve the agaranta in cold water and dissolve the starch in the soy milk. Combine the 2 liquids and bring to a boil. As soon as it boils and the mixture begins to become dense I added salt and lemon juice. Leave to boil for 2 minutes stirring constantly. Then turn off the heat and add the cream with the yogurt. Stir well! Grease the mold or container with oil and pour in the cheese. Leave to cool for a few hours. Then divide the cheese, which will still be solid, into 3 bowls.

b. Flavour each bowl with the ingredients described above (first taste: fresh chopped chives and walnuts for decoration; second taste: squeezed garlic, chilli pepper and sweet paprika; third taste: chopped walnuts, a little squeezed garlic and green apple for decoration). Put in the mixer and blend briefly to obtain a spreadable cheese consistency. 3 bowls 3 flavours Serve as you see fit. I served it in the teaspoons to impress my omnivorous guests.

23. Sottilfette

Ingredients:

- 4½ oz of soft tofu (spoon-type pudding)
- 3/4 cup and 1 teaspoon of water
- 1 teaspoon of coconut oil
- 1 tablespoon mustard in a tube
- 1 teaspoon of filtered lemon juice
- salt
- 1 teaspoonful of locust bean gum (thickener)
- 1 tablespoon of powdered agat agar (Rapunzel)
- 1 teaspoonful of onion paste in a tube
- coconut oil (for greasing the mould)

Procedure:

a. First, let's blend the tofu with the minipimer, until you get a velvety mousse more or less like this. Put the agar agar and the locust bean gum into a jar, add the water (cold) and, after screwing on the lid, shake the jar well until the powders are completely dissolved in the water.

b. At this point, pour the contents of the jar into a cylindrical container, add the tofu mousse and all the other ingredients and then blend everything, trying to get air into the mixture. This is the right time to taste it, to check if it is okay with salt and lemon juice, according to your taste: the secret is to use very small doses, so you are always in time to correct the shot! We transfer the cream cheese into a saucepan and cook it on the stove, over a low heat, stirring continuously with a wooden spoon, until it has reached the boil and assumed a semi-fluid and smooth consistency, like yogurt. We fill with the compound of the moulds greased with coconut oil.

24. Veg Cheese Sage And Walnuts

Ingredients:

- 5 1/3 oz of natural soya yoghurt
- 5 1/3 oz of natural soy milk
- 3 tablespoons of baking powder
- 1¾ oz of chopped walnut kernels
- 1/4 oz of salt
- 3 level tablespoons of cornstarch
- 1 tablespoon evo oil
- 2 tablespoons of seed oil
- 1 sprinkling of dried sage

Procedure:

a. Mix all the ingredients with a whisk to avoid creating lumps. Put on a moderate flame until it hardens, it should not become hard but sticky. Transfer to a bowl greased with oil and leave to cool.

25. Fiordoro

Ingredients:

- 200 dandelion flowers (an average basin of 25 cm in diameter)
- 2/3 cup of unsweetened soy milk
- 1 tablespoon of soya cream
- 3 tablespoons of liego (food yeast in flakes plus pulverized sesame seeds)
- salt, pepper to taste
- 1/3 cup of cold water
- 1 tablespoon of agar agar
- 1 tablespoon of good evo oil
- 1 pinch of marjoram
- 1 pinch of thyme

- 1 teaspoon of lemon juice
- seed oil qb (to grease the mould)

Procedure:

a. First of all, we eliminate the stem, the calyx and the sepals from the still dry flowers, so that only the petals remain, which we will soak in a colander with narrow holes, in order to eliminate any impurities. Then, we put the flowers, drained from the excess water, in a cylindrical and capacious container, then we combine the milk, the cream, 1 pinch of salt and pepper, and we mix everything with the minipimer. After this operation, add also the agar agar dissolved in water and reduced to gel and mix with a spoon, then pour the beautiful golden cream and sliding in a non-stick pot. Turn on the stove at least under the pot and stir continuously until the cream will not reach the boil, then add the flavors, check again if it is fine with salt and let simmer for 2 minutes, no more, before removing the pan from the heat. Add a tablespoon of olive oil raw and stir again gently, incorporating also 1 tablespoon of liego and lemon juice. Finally, after greasing the mould with seed oil and sprinkling it with the 2nd spoonful of liego, pour the mixture into the same container, covering the surface with the remaining liego. Let the cream cheese cool down and then put it in the fridge to solidify for 1 whole night, until it turns into Fiordoro.

26. Tofulivella

Ingredients:

- 11 oz of natural tofu
- 1 tablespoon full of black olive pate
- 1/4 teaspoon of chilli paste
- 1 teaspoon desalted capers
- 3 walnuts
- rind and juice of 1/2 lemon
- a few clumps of parsley
- 2 tablespoons of Evo oil
- 1 teaspoon of dried oregano

Procedure:

a. Boil the tofu for 10 minutes, drain, let it cool and then blend everything! Only add salt if necessary.

27. Tarragon

Ingredients:

- 15 oz of kohlrabi (kcal 115.02, kcal 27/100 g)
- 14 oz of water
- 1 oz of kanten (kcal 4, kcal 16/100 g)
- 3½ oz brewer's yeast (kcal 54, kcal 54/100 g)
- 1½ oz of onion paste (16 kcal, 40/100 g kcal)
- 1/7 oz of gomashio (kcal 17.07, kcal 569/100 g)
- 1 handful of dried tarragon

- 1 pinch of salt
- 1 pinch of pepper
- 1 pinch of assafoetida
- 1 small handful of peppercorns
- little miso red
- little sunflower seed oil

Procedure:
  a. Grate the kohlrabi and put it in the pot. Dissolve the kanten in the water indicated and add to the kohlrabi. Bring to the boil over low heat, adjusting salt and pepper to taste.
  b. Boil for a few minutes until the mixture has thickened and helped with the pancake will leave the walls of the pan clean.
  c. Only last, with the heat off, add the other ingredients except miso and oil. The oil is used only to grease the shape slightly and then sprinkle with a light, just a veil of red miso, the medium-salted one. Then pour in the mixture, sprinkle with tarragon and leave to cool to room temperature without a lid, then in the fridge with a lid.

Considerations:
  a. Tot 873 g cold kcal 206.09, or kcal 23.61/100 g. When you open the container, the smell is strong of cabbage. On tasting, however, the aroma of cabbage is not there and reminds a lot of the Sardinian pecorino semi-cured mountain, what the shepherds do in Barbagia, with rules of cleanliness a bit 'dubious, and that are usually good candidates to become casu marzu (rotten cheese) with lots of jumping worms! Here, of course, there are no worms, the cleanliness has been taken care of to the maximum and the taste is a little more pepose. Looking at the figure, you can see a whitish foam, a sign that the miso, although little, has penetrated the cheese and has slightly fermented. Cacio dragoncello is grated which is a marvel with a hand grater: as I did today at lunch on some shiritake, it looked like pecorino romano! As in the case of pecorino, cacio dragoncello is absolutely a delight spread with a little rice malt: perfect! Today I did an experiment with isolated soy protein. Tomorrow I will do it again because, to become "a fact", the result must be reproducible. If I am successful I will publish it and it will be surprising.

28. Cacilette

Ingredients:

- 1/2 onion
- 1/2 carrot
- 1 piece of celery
- 1 tablespoon chickpea flour
- 1 level tablespoon of coconut oil
- 3/4 cup and 2 tablespoons neutral coconut milk
- 1/3 cup and 1 table spoon of cold water
- 1 level teaspoon of powdered agar

- rosemary
- garlic powder
- nutmeg
- ginger
- chili
- halls
- 1/2 teaspoon of soy sauce

Procedure:

a. Cut the vegetables into small cubes and fry them in a non-stick pot with coconut oil. Add the chickpea flour to toast and then the spices. Now pour the coconut milk and the drop of soy sauce, continuing to turn until you see everything thicken and veil the relatives of the pot. Finally pour the water with the melted agar and continue to cook turning until you reach a consistency like béchamel. Pour it into a rectangular refrigerator container (there is no need to grease it), wait until it reaches room temperature and store it in the refrigerator.

The point:

a. Using coconut milk you get a product that melts while remaining creamy, exactly like the thin slices. It also works in the microwave at low power, but the uses are endless as our imagination! Pizzas, flans, gratins, and whoever has more... the more you eat it! I am dependent on it. I forgot: try to use the coconut milk in the mash, it gives a unique creaminess; and the other evening I added to 200 ml of coconut milk 1 tablespoon of potato starch and poured everything raw over the moussaka before baking it, obtaining a very fast béchamel sauce.

29. Radicamaro

Ingredients:

- 9 oz of already boiled bitter roots of mâche
- 2/3 cup of water or light cold vegetable broth
- 1 clove of garlic (optional)
- 1 tablespoon of powdered agar agar (Rapunzel)
- salt, black pepper to taste
- 1 tablespoon of flakes of food-grade yeast
- 1 tablespoon evo oil
- Seed oil for greasing the mould

Procedure:

a. Nettate and peel the bitter roots and cut them into chunks, then dive them into a pot of boiling water and boil them: it will take 15 minutes. Drain the bitter roots and crush them with a fork, then briefly sauté them in a frying pan of oil and garlic with a pinch of salt. You can skip this step if you don't like garlic, just squeezing the roots. Incorporate the yeast and mix well until you get a thick cream. Dissolve the agar carefully in cold veg water or broth and pour the liquid into a saucepan. Add the root cream and mix well, seasoning with salt and pepper. Put the pan over the sweet heat of the stove and wait for the mixture to boil: at this point, adjusting the heat to the minimum, cook for another 2 minutes, then remove the pan from the heat. Transfer the veg cheese into a previously oiled mould and cover with yeast on the surface if you like. Finally let it cool at room temperature before putting it in the fridge to solidify for 4 hours.

30. Condicacio

Ingredients:

- 1 handful of stoned sweet black olives
- 1 glass (for wine) of tomato puree
- 1/2 glass of cold water
- 1 tablespoon of agar agar powder Rapunzel
- 1 tablespoon evo oil
- salt, pepper to taste
- oregano qb
- chilli to taste

Procedure:

a. Blend the olives with the minipimer, add the puree, salt and herbs and boil the mixture for 10 minutes in a saucepan. Let it cool down. Dissolve the agar well in cold water and pour the gel obtained in the pot. Mix thoroughly (if necessary, mix again) and put the pan back on the heat. When it boils, add the oil and cook for 2 minutes the cream cheese, then pour it into an oiled mold and let the mixture cool down before putting the mold in the fridge for 1 night.

31. Lupis

Ingredients:

- 18 oz of vacuum lupins
- water
- rosemary
- evo oil
- salt, pepper

Procedure:

a. Peel the lupins and keep them soaking for a while. The more they soak, the more they lose salt, I have kept them for about 1/2 hour. Blend them with an immersion blender or a mixer adding a little water at a time, just enough to make them a fairly firm cream like ricotta, I have added 1 tablespoon at a time. If you have not kept them too much soaking do not need to add salt, however, taste the cream. At this point put the cream (which is also great as hummus with the addition of some spice) in a greasy container and leave a few hours in the fridge (I used a cup). Prepare a baking sheet with a small square of baking paper and grease it lightly in the central part where you will place the "formaggino". Turn the container over on the baking paper and drop the form gently. Sometimes it can be deformed, but with your hands you can adjust everything! Lightly grease with your fingers and sprinkle with finely chopped rosemary, pepper and a little salt.

32. Casu

Ingredients:
- 25 oz of thorny artichokes (kcal 268, kcal 47/100 g)
- 3½ oz red onion (kcal 40, kcal 40/100 g)
- 1 ¼ oz parsley (kcal 12.6, kcal 36/100 g)
- 5/7 oz of garlic (kcal 18, kcal 90/100 g)
- ½ oz gomashio (kcal 84.75, kcal 567/100 g)
- turmeric
- black pepper
- water qb
- 1 cup of cold water (or soya buttermilk)
- 5/7 oz of kanten powder (kcal 3.2 4.48, kcal 16/100 g)

Procedure:
a. Clean the artichokes and put in a pot stems and hearts cut into cloves together with the onion, parsley and garlic. Stew the artichokes in water just enough to make them very soft and all the liquid absorbed. Leave to cool, then take 300 g of stewed artichokes to be mixed by immersion until you get a very homogeneous cream. Season the artichoke cream with gomashio and a pinch of turmeric mixed with a little black pepper. Dissolve the kanten carefully in the amount of cold water indicated and pour the gel obtained in the past of artichokes. Continue to cook over a low heat, preferably with a radiant plate to avoid burning the bottom of the pan. When the mixture has reached the boil, thickening, continue cooking for another 2-5 minutes, until it begins to detach from the walls and bottom of the pan. Pour the mixture into a mould greased with oil and sprinkled with gomashio or other flavouring, or nothing. Cover with another pinch of gomashio and let cool to room temperature. Casu Cancioffa is already solid after 1 hour at room temperature, so it is not necessary to refrigerate.

CONCLUSIONS

Excluding foods based on animal proteins generally increases the consumption of plant foods rich in vitamins, minerals and substances with antioxidant power, which is why it is believed that the vegan diet promotes longevity as well as, more generally, health.

Moreover, by completely eliminating foods rich in saturated fats and cholesterol such as those of animal origin, it is possible to prevent certain diseases such as cardiovascular diseases, hypertension, type 2 diabetes and certain cancers.

A good vegan diet can help you lose weight. According to a study presented on the occasion of Obesity Week a few years ago, vegetarians and vegans lose weight more easily than others and can achieve better results; this is because they introduce less saturated fat and calories in their meals, still reaching the feeling of satiety.

When a hand is raised to support the vegan diet, there is always a voice that cries out for vitamin B12 deficiency. In fact, if a vegetarian does not eat meat, he can still find this precious element in milk and eggs.

In the case of a vegan, however, the concern about vitamin B12 becomes real and sensible, because it is a vitamin that plants do not produce. Vitamin B12 comes from the bacteria present in the soil; those who eat only vegetables are forced to wash their food in compliance with essential hygiene standards.

However, these necessary precautions ensure that the external content of the plant, and therefore vitamin B12, is lost during washing. Alternative sources are foods with added vitamins (it is better to prefer those in which the addition is limited to B12) or supplements (also limited to B12, because the other vitamins are obtained from fruit and vegetables).

You can choose to take the vitamin once a week (one 2000 microgram tablet) or daily once a day (one 10 microgram tablet). In fact, even eating meat can lead to vitamin B12 deficiency: not only because some drugs prevent its absorption, but also because it has been found that some organisms of individuals under 50 years of age release that type of vitamin with difficulty.

Another deficiency attributed to the vegan diet is the iron deficiency. In reality, there is much more iron in a vegetable-based diet than in an omnivorous diet, especially if you combine vegetables with fruit, tomatoes or foods rich in vitamin C.

Iron deficiency anemia contrasts with legumes, cereals, leafy vegetables. Finally, foods that are rich in fiber are also foods that contain more iron. To give a simple example: horse meat contains 3.9 milligrams of iron per hundred grams; legumes contain more than twice as much.

All-vegetable nutrition provides our bodies with more fiber, antioxidants and vitamins, which, when taken in the right proportions, help us combat fatigue, free radicals and stress.

The vegan diet is an automatic defense against bacterial diseases that can result from bad farming, slaughtering and preservation of meat from both terrestrial and marine species. Products from large farms can also be contaminated with bacteria, antibiotics and toxins. Not to mention the widespread use of hormones with which animals are bred.

Those who eat food of animal origin will only accumulate these harmful elements in the body. Over the years, this could lead to increased resistance to antibiotics, metabolic damage, inflammation and cancer.

Those who want to adopt a vegan diet must in any case pay attention to the origin and quality of the raw materials. In fact, products treated with insecticides and pesticides often banned by the European Union should be avoided. For this reason, we at Naturveg only purchase the raw materials for our supplements from Italian and European suppliers who have all the necessary certifications.

The reasons behind a vegan diet, in any case, are not reduced only to a question of the general health of the individual. But they include other economic, ecological and social aspects. When judged by all these nuances, the vegan choice is undoubtedly the most suitable diet for a sustainable lifestyle for oneself and for others.

The second most common criticism, after that of nutritional deficiencies, advanced to the vegan diet is not to take into account the hectares of land used in agriculture for the production of legumes, particularly soybeans. Yet it is enough to take a very simple figure to be able to dismantle this position and show that the vegan diet is also the most sustainable from an ecological point of view.

FAO figures estimate that more than 60 billion animals are slaughtered each year by the food industry, of which more than 7.5 billion are slaughtered in the European Union alone. These statistics also exclude the incredible number of fish and other aquatic species that are caught or bred each year.

Let's feed well, our body is our temple.

Finally, if you found this book useful in any way, a review on Amazon is always appreciated!